AF529410

FINANCIAL REFORMS AND NEW DEVELOPMENT IN BANKS

FINANCIAL REFORMS AND NEW DEVELOPMENT IN BANKS

S. Chinnammai
R. Kanaka Sudha

SERIALS PUBLICATIONS
NEW DELHI (INDIA)

© S. Chinnammai & R. Kanaka Sudha

First Published – 2010

ISBN: 978-81-8387-267-6

All rights reserved with the Publisher, including the right to translate or reproduce this book or parts there of except for brief quotations in critical articles or reviews.

Published by

SERIALS PUBLICATIONS
4800/24, 1st Floor, Ansari Road
Darya Ganj, New Delhi-110002 (India)
Phone : 23245225. Fax : 91-11-23272135
E-mail: serials@satyam.net.in

CONTENTS

FOREWORD

The New Economic Policy introduced by the Government of India in 1991 has brought about a sea- change in the Financial Sector in the country. Several developments, which were, at one time, considered unthinkable, took place in India in the financial as well as other sectors as a consequence of the New Economic Policy of 1991. The birth of New Generation Private Sector Banks, step by step opening of the country's economy, a more liberal exchange control regime, easier access for the private sector to external commercial borrowings and a more benign approach to Foreign Investment in India are some examples. These developments were accompanied by the advent of new Financial Products & Services.

Though Credit Card, as a financial product, has been in existence in the country since the 80's, it was only after the introduction of the New Economic Policy of 1991 that Credit Cards literally took wings and became well known to a large section of the Indian society as a payment mechanism. Till then, it was considered as something meant only for the elite. The growth of the Cards Industry during the last two decades has been so substantial that cards are today accepted as a payment mechanism even in remote corners of the country and the number of cardholders and card users has grown from a few lakhs prior to 1991 to several crores in 2009.

Though cards have now come to be accepted as a major payment mechanism, hardly any authentic, published information is available even today for someone who is keen to understand what the credit cards business is all about. This book, written by Dr. (Mrs.) S. Chinnammai and Ms. Kanaka

Sudha, which discusses the Impact of the New Economic Policy of 1991 and new developments in banks with special reference to Credit Cards System, is a first of its kind, providing substantial information about the Credit Card Industry. It attempts to fill the void which has all along been felt by many a student of Finance & Financial Services keen to lay hands on an authentic source of information on Credit Cards Business. This book is a product of the extensive research carried out by Dr. (Mrs.) S. Chinnammai and Ms. R. Kanaka Sudha. The book contains substantial statistical data on various aspects of Cards Business in India. Though the book covered the financial reforms and new development in banks, a major part of the book is devoted to the new developments of Cards Business in banks in general in India and the World as a whole. As such, any student keen to acquire knowledge about the credit cards business will find the book extremely useful and can benefit enormously from the study of this book.

This book can be considered a milestone in credit cards business which throws a path for new research for multi-dimensional analyses in the field of all types of card business in banks. In the globalized economy, this book will be useful as a future guide for card business. Though this book is like candlelight in the dark on the credit card business, it goes a long way in fulfilling the need for a single source of information on all aspects of the credit cards business. This book is a tribute to the perseverance and hard working nature of its authors in having undertaken a study of this magnitude and bringing out a book of high quality.

Personally, I would recommend this book as a study material for students of Financial Services and all those who are in any way associated with the cards industry and are keen to know more about it.

N. GOPALAKRISHNAN
Vice President-Cards Operations
HDFC Bank Limited, Cards Division Chennai

Place: Chennai
Date: 16/02/2009

ACKNOWLEDGEMENTS

First and foremost, we would like to thank **Dr. Duraisamy**, Lecturer in Economics, Madras Christian College, for the guidance given in getting an insight in the subject and **Dr. Ravanan**, Reader in Statistics, Presidency College, without whose guidance our statistical works would have been incomplete. We also express our deep sense of gratitude to **Dr. T. Prabha**, Dean (Retd.), Lady Doak College, Madurai, who constantly guided us for completing this study.

Our sincere thanks to **Mr. Gopalakrishnan**, Vice President–Credit Cards Operation, Cards Division, HDFC Bank Limited, in securing information about the study and providing valuable guidance in every step for the proper course of this study. We also extend our heartiest thanks to all Heads of Credit Card Division of various banks, without whose co-operation, this study would not have been quite extensive.

Our thanks are also due to **Mr. T. S. Sridhar**, Vice President, International Sales, Versatile Card Technology, who helped us in furnishing details pertaining to the study and helped us in arranging for meetings with higher authorities in banks connected to credit card sector, without whose help, obtaining data from various sources would have been impossible. Our gratefulness is due to **Mr. S. Raj Vikram**, Owner, SLIM (Sound Light Image Magic) Studios.

Last but not least, our gratitude to personnel of Versatile Card Technology for their extended support and guidance.

ABBREVIATIONS

AMEX	American Express Bank
ATM	Automated Teller Machine
BOB	Bank of Baroda
BOI	Bank of India
CBI	Central Bank of India
CRY	Child Relief and You
ECS	Electronic Clearing Service
EOU	Export Oriented Units
EU	European Union
EXIM	Export-Import Policy
FDI	Foreign Direct Investments
FII	Foreign Investments in India
HDFC	Housing Development and Finance Corporation
HSBC	Hong Kong and Shanghai Banking corporation
ICICI	Industrial Credit and Investment Corporation of India
ICMA	International Card Manufacturers' Association
IDBI	Industrial Development Bank of India IMF International Monetary Fund
J&K Bank	Jammu & Kashmir Bank
MNC	Multinational Companies
MRTP	Monopolies and Restrictive Trade Practices Act

NCAER	National Council of Applied Economic Research
NEP	New Economic Policy
PAN	Permanent Account Number
PIN	Personal Identification Number
PNB	Punjab National Bank
PSB	Public Sector Bank
RBI	Reserve Bank of India
SBI	State Bank of India
SEBI	Stock Exchange Board of India
STANCHART	Standard Chartered Bank
U.K.	United Kingdom
U.S.	United States of America
UTI	Unit Trust of India (now called Axis Bank)
WWF	World Wildlife Fund

GLOSSARY OF TERMS

Acquirer	A financial institution that supports merchants by providing services for processing card transactions.
American Express	An organization that issues cards and acquires transactions (unlike visa and MasterCard, which are bank associations).
Authorization	Approval by or on behalf of the card issuer to validate the transactions for a merchant or another affiliate bank.
Automated Teller	An unmanned electronic device that performs basic machine teller function such as accepting deposits, cash Withdrawals and account balance enquiries.
Bank	An institution that handles savings and current accounts, issues loans and credit, deals in government/corporation issued securities.
Credit card	A bank issued card that allows consumers to purchase goods or services on credit.
Internet	A global network of networks. The internet supports many services such as email updated news, remote login and file transfers
Issuer	Provider of a bank card to a cardholder and authorizing that person to use it to complete financial transactions.

MasterCard	An association of banks that governs the issuing and acquiring of MasterCard credit card transactions.
Merchant	A retailer, or any other entity (pursuant to a merchant agreement), that agrees to accept credit cards, debit cards or both, when properly presented.
Online	A computer or user is online when connected to a network or server that allows communication flow between computers.
PIN	Personal identification number used as a password to gain access to bank or credit accounts. It is required to perform financial transactions using a debit or credit card.
POS	Point of sale. The place and time at which a transaction occurs. This term also refers to the devices or software used to capture transactions.
Transaction Fee	A "per transaction" charge incurred by merchants who are on scale pricing. This is in addition to the percentage discount fees.
VISA	An association of banks that governs the issuing and acquiring of visa card transactions.

1

INTRODUCTION

"Our primary concerns are that globalization should benefit all countries and should raise the welfare of all people throughout the world...."–World Commission on the Social Dimension of Globalization (2004)[1]. The word "globalization" itself shows that the world is witnessing development in the international arena–a trend towards increasing economic interdependence of global markets. The aim of globalization was that of working as a single identity by the global markets, produce goods and services more efficiently and at a comparatively lower cost, utilizing the resource availabilities of the respective countries, (including information technologies too), be it capital intensive or labour intensive, and thereby have an equitable distribution of the same to attain competitive advantage.

Thus, basically globalization signifies a process of internationalization plus liberalization. It had a rippling effect throughout the world. There were arguments for and against globalization. And, India was one among the many countries which adopted the advocacy of globalization, liberalization and privatization of the developed countries. India has been, in the past decades, and is still a live participant in the dynamic Science and Technology transformation of the world. It has adopted varieties of strategies in the global participation including augmentation of educational and research infrastructure, import of technologies from developed countries and indigenization of such imported ones.[2]

CRISIS IN THE 80'S LEADING TO ADVENT OF NEW ECONOMIC POLICY (NEP), 1991 AND GLOBALISATION

In 1985, a series of moves amounted to an expansive, debt-dependent fiscal policy directed at stimulating the growth of the economy. The changes covered all the major fields of regulation except the capital market. The rigour of Monopolies and Restrictive Trade Practices Act, (MRTP) (1969) was considerably reduced. The government encouraged foreign investment into many areas. It liberalized the imports of capital goods and materials, especially those needed for large projects. The government restored to higher and higher doses of deficit financing to defray its expenditures. By 1991, India was faced with the prospect of defaulting of her debt obligations, unable even to secure short term loans. In JUNE-JULY 1991, in order to restore confidence among India's debtors and in the rupee, the government entered into an agreement with the IMF. The rupee was devalued by 24%. Quantitative Restrictions on imports were moderated. Foreign financial institutions were allowed to enter the stock market. A series of reforms were undertaken in all aspects of the economy–Industrial Reforms, Economic Reforms, Financial Sector Reforms, Banking Reforms, Trade Reforms are the most important ones to be mentioned.

ECONOMIC REFORMS

The Eighth Five Year Plan (1992-1997) was launched in the backdrop of momentous changes in the world and India. The NEP 1991 had recognized that in many areas of activity, development can be best ensured by freeing them of unnecessary controls and regulations. At the same time, it was realized that planning is necessary for macro-economic management. With the increased liberalization of the economy, planning became indicative in nature. It consisted of building a long term strategic view of the future and set forth the priorities of the nation.

INDUSTRIAL REFORMS

Initially, in this sector, there were various controls like the industrial licensing system, reservation of certain industries and time consuming procedures. But with the advent of NEP 1991, this sector was liberalized from various reservations and procedures. A drastic change occurred in the Export-Import (EXIM) Policy. A thrust to exports was given, import duties were reduced substantially in subsequent budgets, Export Oriented Units (EOU) were promoted, duty free imports allowed for exports, to mention a few. Another aspect of this new industrial policy was the virtual scrapping of the license system. In cases of foreign companies, in some cases, there were provision for the 'automatic' approval of license applications. The objective was to set up a deregulated industrial economy, largely operated by the private sector, or both indigenous and foreign origin. From May 1992, Foreign Investors in India (FII) were allowed to participate directly in the Indian stock market. The BJP-led central government had allowed foreigners to hold 100% equity stake in most sector of industry and services. After the revelation of the Bank Scam in May, 1992 (Securities Scam by Harshad Mehta), India decided to endow the Stock Exchange Board of India (SEBI - established in 1988), with some real powers of monitoring and regulating the stock markets.

FINANCIAL/BANKING SECTOR REFORMS

Financial System forms a significant part of the infrastructure essential for breaking the vicious circle of poverty. Schumpeter spoke of credit as a "phenomenon of development" and regarded the banking system along with entrepreneurship as being the key agent in the process of development. The role of banking in economic development is one of positive contribution which ignites the growth and pattern of evolution of the banking structure. The Indian banking system has passed through distinct phases of development after independence.[3] The first phase can be attributed to the nationalization of 14 banks on July 19, 1969 (and another 6 banks in 1980). Nationalization of banks was described as 'historic', 'momentous' and 'bold' and 'timely' by some economists while it was vehemently criticized as wrong and untimely by others. In defense of her view, Mrs. Indira Gandhi, the then Prime Minister of India, argued that the Indian Commercial Banking

System did not play its proper role in the planned development of the nation. According to her, the banking system was controlled by a coterie of industrialist and business magnates who had used public funds to build up private industrial empires. Small industrial and business units were continuously and consistently ignored and hence the nationalization of banks.[4] Beginning 1969, the second phase can be attributed to the diversification of the banking system in terms of expansion and social banking; the third phase being attributed to the advent of NEP, 1991, which gave a further impetus to this sector.

The then Congress government had appointed on August 14, 1991, a committee under the chairmanship of Shri M. Narasimhan to examine all aspects relating to the structure, organization, functions and procedures of the financial system. The committee submitted its final report to the government on November 16, 1991. The committee had noted that deterioration in the financial health of the system had reached a point where unless remedial measures were taken soon, it would further erode the confidence of the depositors and investors. Many major recommendations were made for the improvement of the banking sector in their various segments, areas of concern were pointed, and an agenda of reforms to be immediately implemented by the banks were suggested. Some of the major policy reforms introduced in the banking sector, in brief, were the following : prudential norms introduced in banks, imparting greater transparency, financial autonomy for nationalized banks announced, new set of private sector banks were allowed to function and more foreign banks allowed to open branches, local area banks proposal was cleared for implementation, bank branch licensing were liberalized, customer service in banking sector was perceived as an integral part of overall reforms, 25 core recommendations of GOIPURIA COMMITTEE report had been implemented, banks were allowed to set up Automated Teller Machines (ATMs) to provide financial facilities, separate department set up for banking supervision. A major effort was made to strengthen the banking systems in general and public sector banks in particular through measures of capitalization, quality of loan portfolio, greater element of competition and strengthening of supervisory process.

With all the above reforms and more reforms in other sectors too, India was put on to the road of globalization, adopting it as an economic policy. Also to attract foreign direct investments (FDI) to India, adoption of globalization, liberalization and privatization became necessary since it found examples in countries like Taiwan, Singapore and Thailand, which had attracted foreign investments by adopting the policy of globalization.

NEW ECONOMIC POLICY (NEP) AND TECHNOLOGY

NEP comprised of various policy measures and changes that were introduced since July 1991. The objectives of these measures were to improve the efficiency of the system. Towards this aim, *the policy permitted free import of technology.* Liberalization had led to subsidiaries of foreign firms and Indian collaborators becoming perpetually dependant on external suppliers of technology. Thus the process of liberalization led to the import of technology thereby facilitating substantial exports. Hence upgradation of technology had become part and parcel of economic development of the country.[5]

IMPACT OF GLOBALISATION IN INDIA

As the name suggests, it means making the Indian economy responsive to the developments taking place at the global level and trying to play greater role in the world economic development. Therefore, it essentially means a free flow of factors of production, goods and services, labour and capital across the globe without any government restrictions.

Globalization reforms aimed at putting our economy in line with the rest of the world and make it conducive for foreign investments. It indicates the desire to integrate the nation – states within the overall framework of the World Trade Organization (WTO). It has four parameters namely, reduction of trade barriers so as to perform free flow of goods across national frontiers, creation of an environment in which free flow of capital can take place among countries, setting up a policy and administrative regime facilitating *free flow of technology,* and clearing the decks for free movement of labour among various countries of the world.

ROLE OF INNOVATION AND TECHNOLOGY

"The key process in the economic force of changes is the introduction of innovation and culture of innovation in the enterprise" described Schumpeter. The innovation process is seen as a cycle involving trial and error, where problems, at some stage of development lead to the need of re-evaluation of the earlier stage of innovation process. This innovation, technology and know-how play a vital role in the growth of any economy.

It was realized that infusion of technology would bring about a change in the delivery format of product and services; an application of technology that has the capacity to change the speed of transactions for such delivery of products and services. And then came the EVOLUTION OF PLASTIC MONEY–a way of purchasing by credit.

Purchasing by credit may seem like a relatively new idea, or at least an early 19th century concept, but actually the history of credit predates the use of money. As far back as 1750 B.C., in ancient Babylonia, farmers were known to borrow seed on the premise that the debt would be paid after the harvest was reaped.

The truly radical notion was the introduction of the credit card and its evolution from a paper process to a metal plate and finally to a plastic component that is as smart as it is durable.

Today's world witness man on the move... in that, there is so much to be done in so little a time. People have evolved to become a more demanding lot with a significant rise in purchasing power. This scenario presents a dynamic market that has pretty much to offer to the discerning customer..., where and how he wants it, and precisely, when he wants it. With rapid strides in technology and commerce shrinking the globe to size, day-to-day transactions happen at the speed of light–by the hour and by the minute–thereby demanding a well organized framework of business that would provide for greater interactions with the customer in meeting or exceeding his expectations and requirements. And, thus has evolved the all-important plastic card that has taken our civilization by storm in redefining business transactions across the globe, empowering the buyer with unprecedented potential that was hitherto unthinkable.[6]

PRIVATISATION, LIBERALIZATION AND BANKS

With the Narasimhan Committee Report, banking system in India turned its gear into a more market-disciplined one. The focus had turned to more profits, fee-based incomes had become more attractive and to increase competition, their efficiency and productivity had to be improved at large. With globalization of business, banks had to prepare for meeting the risks from international banking which increased with liberalization. Thus entered the banking sector reforms into the third phase of INNOVATIVE BANKING[7], as stated earlier. Of the various forms of innovations in the Indian banking system consisted the following namely, new technology in banking mechanization, wherein the Electronic Clearing Service (ECS) got an impetus, improvement in the level of customer satisfaction to reach efficiency, banking Ombudsman for expeditious and inexpensive settlement of customer complaints against deficiency in banking services, installations of ATMs where clients can withdraw cash 24 hours a day upto a certain limit, CREDIT CARDS which now forms an integral part of better customer service.

Under the credit scheme, card holders are allowed credit facilities for a specified period of time without obtaining any security from them. The card holders can purchase commodities and pay for services without making cash payments immediately. The bank issuing the credit card is able to make increased earnings by way of commission from dealers and interest from card holders. This has become an aggressive area of business for Indian banks. Major public sector and private sector banks have come out with their credit cards. Some of them have been permitted by the RBI to have tie-up arrangements with other banks in India and abroad. This has facilitated wider use of cards nationally and internationally.

SEGMENT PERFORMANCE OF CREDIT CARD INDUSTRY

India is the only country in the Asia-Pacific region that has registered a double-digit growth in the credit card segment. The growth rate has maintained the momentum for the last four years and is expected to continue at the same rate. The plastic culture is influencing into the daily purchasing habits of Indian consumers, and the payment card business is growing as never before.

As it happened elsewhere, traditionally the consumer has begun with patronizing credit cards. Therefore credit cards comprise the bulk of payment cards in India.

ECONOMY DRIVING SPENDS

A thriving economy, with substantial increase in disposable incomes and consequent rise in consumer expenditure, growing affluence levels and consumer sophistication have all led to a robust growth in credit cards and each player have posted an enviable annual growth rate of more than 100% over the last 2 years.[8]

TIMELINE AT THE BIRTH OF THE CARD

This condensed timeline shows us the roll-out of an idea that breathed new life into commerce and economics and introduced the concept of "Buy Now, Pay Later" and "Just Charge it".

1914 Retail shops issue paper prototype of charge card to wealthy customers.

1920 First official payment card called the Shopper's plate issued in USA.

1926 B.F. Goodrich, chemist Waldo Semon develops plastic.

1930 Banks and other business institutions consider the validity and effectiveness of the emerging credit card.

1936 Retail Service Bureau of Seattle signs up 1,000 establishments that agree to honor each other's charge cards and an itemized monthly bill covering all items.

1939 Standard Oil of Indiana issues 2,50,000 credit cards to roll out its first major card marketing campaign.

1947 John Biggins, banker and consumer credit specialist, drafts a plan that ultimately becomes the universal credit card.

1949 Frank X. McNamara and associates conceive the first official credit card. This eventually became a DINERS CLUB CARD, now owned by Citigroup.

1952 The Franklin National Bank of New York establishes the first bank credit card.

1955 Bank Cards increase popularity, with more than 100 types available on the market.

1958 The Bank Americard is introduced. The AMERICAN EXPRESS enters the universal credit card arena.

1959 AMERICAN EXPRESS introduces the first plastic charge card.

1965 BHR of Great Britain and Rikskort of Sweden form EUROCARD INTERNATIONAL.

ATM introduced at the American Bankers' Association Automation Conference.

1968 MAGNETIC STRIPE is developed by IBM for storing information on a credit card.

1969 Continental Bank purchases the Diners Club Card.

1971 COUNTERFEIT CREDIT CARDS are reported for the first time in Los Angeles.

1972 The FEDERAL RESERVE BOARD becomes the premier regulatory body for the credit industry.

1976 Bank of America changes card name to VISA.

1977 Equal Credit Opportunity becomes law, barring the use of race, color, creed, gender, national origin or marital status as criteria for issuing or denying credit.

1980 Master charge becomes MASTERCARD.

1984 Bank Cards experience enormous popularity.

1999 Consumers can transfer credit card information securely over the internet with the American Express Chip–embedded Blue Card.

2001 157 million Americans in the U.S. own credit cards.

2004 Over 8.8 billion plastic cards are issued globally[9].

2007 India alone produces over 100 billion cards for its global supply.[10]

CHARACTERISTIC FEATURES OF A CREDIT CARD

A Credit Card possesses certain characteristic features which are as follows: it is easy to carry and hold, there is freedom of choice to the customer with respect to his spending pattern, flexible repayment of installment credit availed under the extended credit facility, different from the other type of credits in the sense there is no guarantee, down payment or pledging of assets required for obtaining a card, freedom on choice of issuer, better substitute to other modes of payment, no immediate dent on savings unlike debit cards, acts as an immediate cash payment during times of emergency or times of shortage of cash in the hands of the consumer.

OVERALL ASSESSMENT

A growing field of NUMISMATICS (Study of Money), or more specifically EXONUMIA (study of money-like objects), credit card collectors seek to collect various embodiments of credit from the now familiar plastic cards to older paper merchant cards, and even metal tokens that were accepted as merchant credit cards. Early credit cards were made of celluloid, then metal and fibre, then paper and are now mostly PLASTIC.

SCOPE OF THE STUDY

Cards seem to be replacing paper work. Credit card gives one credit for a whole lot of things, debit card enables one to shop practically with an empty wallet, discount card helps one to strike the best bargain, privilege card makes one an exclusive person, identity card distinguishes a person, voter card turns one a responsible citizen of the country and PAN CARD certifies one as an assessee.

Imagine a person travelling, with probing mind, tension-filled with questions like keeping the cash safely to fulfill his various needs, how much to carry to unfamiliar places, how safe it is, whether the amount being carried is sufficient enough until the end of the travel etc. cropping. For all such queries, credit card provides an answer. In today's world, the general perspective itself is totally different from that of a generation before. With the card culture in vogue, it becomes inevitable to study the various functions of the credit card–A MATTER OF SWIPE.

This study has been attempted in order to highlight the basic utilities of Credit Cards, in the background of the consumer's age, qualification and financial freedom in the fast changing economic scenario. With the advent of globalization and liberalization policies in India since 1991, the consumer has a variety of goods and services to choose between the flooded market of various brands and qualities, increasing his/her purchasing and bargaining power. The study has also attempted to highlight the importance of credit card usage as it might lead to a debt trap.

For the second dimension, to make the study more appropriate, merchant establishments' perspective of accepting credit cards has also been tried to visualize, to provide a better understanding of the impact of credit cards due to liberalized economy.

To give the study a more sharper angle, the third dimension of banks' perspective has also been analyzed, they being the major issuers of credit cards to consumers, (and in India, the sole issuers of credit cards) and how, after the 1991 New Economic Policy, banking sector underwent major changes and how Credit Cards started playing a critical role in retail banking sector of the bank and how banks were able to make more profits due to this sector alongside catering to customer satisfaction.

OBJECTIVES OF THE STUDY

The objectives of the study are as follows:

(1) To study the global scenario with respect to credit card system.

(2.) To analyze the scope of credit card system in Asia-Pacific region.

(3) To examine the economic and financial reforms in India with particular reference to the credit card system prevailing in India.

(4) To find out the relationship between holding of credit card and consumer behaviour in Chennai city.

(5) To examine the impact of globalization on credit card acceptance from merchant's view.

(6) To study the financial reforms in the banking sector as an issuer of credit cards in the economy.

(7) To find out the future role of credit cards in the economy.

(8) To find out ways and means for better functioning of credit cards in the banking sector.

(9) To suggest some policy measures and future growth of the economy through better working methods of credit card system in India.

RESEARCH METHOD AND MEHTODOLOGY

A research method may be understood as all those methods employed for conduction of research. In this study, to know the background of the Credit Card industry, its growing importance and its relevance to India and Chennai city in particular, historical research for obtaining information for the above has been employed. In order to know the current situation and trend, survey method, in the form of questionnaire and personal interaction has been employed.

Research Methodology is a way to systematically solve the research problem. The methodology adopted in this study includes various statistical tools as per the requirements of the data and information for which the study is conducted.

SOURCES OF INFORMATION

The study is primarily based on data collected from two sources:

(1) Secondary data and

(2) Primary data.

SECONDARY DATA

For obtaining the background of this Credit Card System and to know the current trend, various sources of secondary data were also collected for the study which included various Reserve Bank of India Bulletins and Summary of the Reports which furnished first hand information about India. With respect to the global scenario, various International Journals were referred which also contained information about the emerging market of India apart from the global market. Moreover, all monthly, weekly and daily newspapers and magazines were browsed through which came up with various articles pertaining to the study and relevant information quoted in appropriate places with reference. Various research surveys, especially the Venture Infotek Research Publication; the only of its kind in India which provides detailed information about the Payments Card Industry on the whole was also referred. Apart from the above, relevant information from internet has also been widely used in the study.

PRIMARY DATA

Collection of data has been through Sampling Method and the method of sampling used was purposive sampling. By purposive sampling is meant sampling done with a purpose in mind. The researcher adopting this method usually has one or more specific predefined groups to be sought. Those whom the market researcher feels will fall under this group, will be sought after and asked whether they can be questioned. Since the purpose of this study focused on the impact of various reforms on the economy after the NEP 1991 through credit cards, only those possessing credit cards in the area of study concerned were selected.

Initially, a pilot survey was conducted for consumers and merchants in order to identify problems, if any, in the questionnaires, for them to answer, or questions that would be overlapping, confusing or delicate for answering and suitable modifications undertaken in the questionnaires before the final survey.

The sample consisted of a cross-section of credit card holders in Chennai City. Individual credit card holders in Chennai City have been chosen for study since it is one of the biggest metropolitan cities in our country where credit card culture is catching up fast.

Chennai City has been analyzed by demarcating it into 4 different categories of East, West, North, South and the method of purposive random sampling has been applied for the survey. To have more consistency in analysis, interpretation and results, the sample size of 150 customers, 75 merchant establishments and leading banks which produce credit cards in Chennai city and/or which has a major market share in the industry has been obtained through the QUESTIONNAIRE METHOD. For this 3 sets of questionnaires were prepared to have a three dimensional analysis.

Various individuals from different parts of Chennai city were approached personally and opinions gained through the Customer Questionnaire schedule and also orally obtained for delicate issues.

Similarly various merchant establishments were approached personally and opinions obtained through the Merchant Questionnaire schedule. Here too, certain personal and intricate information regarding credit cards, banks' approach, terminals used etc were obtained by interviewing them orally.

Various Bank Managers heading the Credit Card Division in Chennai City were met and interviewed to gain knowledge of the working of the Credit Card System and using the questionnaire schedule pertaining to banks.

UNIVERSE

Though Chennai city has a population of more than 4.2 million, as per 2001 Census, only a sample size of 150 customers and 75 Merchant Establishments in Chennai has been taken into consideration for the study. Similarly, though there are many banks, only those producing credit cards in Chennai and holding a major market share has been considered. Hence of few such handful of banks, 7 banks were approached for survey. Since credit card involves the user, issuer and the acceptor of goods and services, all the three were simultaneously considered since all of them play an equal and important role for the functioning of the system as such. The researcher has felt that no dimension influencing the effective working of the credit card system should be left out and hence equal importance has been given to consumers who are the ultimate users, merchants who are the acceptors of credit cards in place of cash when approached for demand for goods and services and the banks who are the ultimate and the sole producers of credit cards in India.

AREA OF STUDY

Though areas were demarcated into 4 different strata of East, West, North and South, samples were selected using the purposive random sampling method. Only those who possessed a credit card were approached for the purpose of this study.

DATA COLLECTION INSTRUMENT

Structured questionnaires were used for the survey. The questionnaires were divided into two different sections. Section I consisted of basic questions to obtain some necessary/ personal information which plays an important role on the impact of Credit Cards in the economy in general. The questionnaire had mostly close ended questions.

Section II consisted of statements based on Likert Scale of five degrees to obtain the behavior, attitude, utility, satisfaction, likely growth potential of credit cards and the like based on the study.

Three sets of questionnaires in the above stated format were prepared, one each for Customers, Merchants and Banks.

STATISTICAL TOOLS EMPLOYED

For analyzing various relationships, economic theories that had traces of similarity in the study and the following statistical tools have been applied in appropriation to the need of data.

(1) *Economic Theories:* Various economic variables that were correlating to the course of study had been applied like the Marshall's Diminishing Marginal Utility, Ando Modigliani's Life Cycle Hypothesis, Keynes' marginal propensities to save and consume, Deusenberry's Demonstration effect etc.

(2) *Arithmetic Mean and Standard Deviation:* The Arithmetic Mean is a common measure for central tendency and may be defined as the value which we get by dividing the total of the value of various given items in a series by the total number of items. The formula for the same is as under :

$$\bar{x} = \frac{\Sigma xi}{n}$$

where $\bar{x}$ = mean

x_i = $x_1 + x_2 + \ldots + x_n$

S = the symbol of summation

x_i = value of the ith item, i = 1, 2, ..., n

n = total number of items

Standard Deviation is the most widely used measure of dispersion denoted by the symbol (σ), pronounced as sigma. It is defined as the square root of the average of deviations. The formula is as under:

$$\text{Standard Deviation } (\sigma) = \sqrt{\frac{\Sigma\,(xi - \bar{x})^2}{n}} \quad \text{for individual items}$$

(or)

$$\text{Standard Deviation}(\sigma) = \sqrt{\frac{\Sigma f_i \ (xi - \bar{x})^2}{\Sigma f_i}}$$ where f_i = frequency of the ith item, in case of frequency distribution.

(3) *Anova (Analysis of Variance):* Developed by Prof. R.A. Fisher, is used to test the differences among the means of the populations by examining the amount of variation within each of these samples, relative to the amount of variation between the samples. The said estimates are compared with F-test wherein.

$$F = \frac{\text{Estimation of population variance based on between samples variance}}{\text{Estimation of population variance based on within samples variance}}$$

This value of F is to be compared to the F-limit for given degrees of freedom.

(4) *Factor Analysis:* This statistical procedure is used to uncover relationships among variables. This allows numerous variables to be condensed into fewer dimensions called factors.

This tool has been employed to know the impact of various factors affecting or contributing to the growth, usage and utility functions of credit cards. Also a specific factor which has a high level of effect on credit cards in the study has been observed and analyzed.

(5) *Hypothesis Testing Using Students t-Test:* This test is considered as an appropriate test for judging the significance of difference between the means of two samples. In case two samples are related, we use paired t-test (or what is known as difference test) for judging the significance of the mean of difference between two related samples.

To test the significance of various independent factors on the dimension and impact on credit cards, this test has been employed in the study. The relevant test statistic, t, is given below which is calculated from the sample data and then compared with its probable value based on t-distribution at a specified level of significance for concerning degrees of freedom for accepting or rejecting the null hypothesis.

$$t \sim \frac{\left|\bar{x} - \mu\right|}{\sigma_s / \sqrt{n}} \text{ with (n – 1) degrees of freedom}$$

$$\text{where } \sigma_s = \sqrt{\frac{\Sigma\left(x_i - \bar{x}\right)^2}{n - 1}}$$

(6) *Chi-Square Test:* Symbolically written as y^2 (pronounced as Ki-Square), is a statistical measure used in the context of sampling analysis for comparing a variance to a theoretical variance. It can be used to determine if categorical data shows dependency or the two classifications are independent.

To test the association between independent factors to their significance level, this tool has been employed in this study using the formula

$$\psi^2 = \frac{\Sigma\, [O_{ij} - E_{ij}]^2}{E_{ij}} \quad i = 1, 2, 3 \ldots$$

$$j = 1, 2, 3 \ldots$$

Where O_{ij} = observed frequency of the cell in i^{th} row and j^{th} column

E_{ij} = Expected frequency of the cell in i^{th} row and j^{th} column

(7) *Correlation Analysis:* Developed by Karl Pearson, this relative measure is known as the co-efficient of correlation (r). This is the most commonly used measure given by the formula

$$r = \Sigma \frac{\left(X_i - \bar{X}\right)\left(Y_i - \bar{Y}\right)}{n \cdot \sigma_X\, \sigma_Y} \text{ where}$$

X_i - i^{th} value of X variable

$\bar{X}$ - mean of X

Y_i - i^{th} value of Y variable

$\bar{Y}$ - mean of y

n - number of pairs of observations of X and Y

σ_X - Standard Deviation of X

σ_Y - Standard Deviation of Y[11]

This method has been employed to know whether there is a positive or negative relationship and whether thereby the variables are directly or inversely correlated. The above mentioned tools have been employed in the study for analyses of collected data in Chapter V.

HYPOTHESES TESTED

(1) There is no significant difference between age group with respect to the impact of credit card usage.

(2) There is no significant difference between occupations with respect to the impact of credit card usage.

(3) There is no significant difference between educational qualification and credit card usage

(4) There is no significant difference between monthly income with respect to the impact of credit card usage.

(5) There is no significant difference between the type of card owned and usage of credit cards.

(6) There is no significant difference between comfortable payments with respect to dimension of credit card usage.

(7) There is no association between educational qualification and type of card preferred to use by respondents.

(8) There is no association between monthly income and type of card preferred to use.

(9) There is no significant difference between various choices in a basket of goods and the preference to use credit cards.

(10) There is no significant difference between acceptance of credit cards and other modes of payment by merchants in the sellers' market.

11. There is no significant difference between the nature of business and credit card acceptance by the merchants.

12. There is no difference between the issuer of credit cards (in this case, only the banks are applicable since they are the only issuers) and the acceptance of credit cards by the merchants.

LIMITATIONS OF THE STUDY

(1) Though the culture of plastic money is widespread throughout India, this study is restricted to Chennai City only, taking into due consideration, time, money and mobility involved.

(2) The study is restricted to the aspect of Credit Cards only. Debit Cards, ATM Cards, Smart Cards and any other similar type of card do not come under the purview of this study since considering every type may involve a wide range of aspects.

(3) To obtain the underlying attitude of the people in various walks of life, be it a consumer, merchant or banking personnel, however, a basic query regarding a credit card and a debit card has just been included in the respective questionnaires.

(4) Chennai city is very vast and has areas in all the four directions. The study has taken only 150 samples for Consumers, 75 samples for Merchant Establishments and 7 major banks using purposive random sampling method.

(5) Only the general opinion of the card issuing banks has been taken into consideration with respect to Credit Cards. Debit Cards or other similar cards do not come under the purview of this study.

(6) The study has not focused on the profit rate or the financial matters of Credit Cards with respect to banks.

(7) There might be a bias on the part of the consumers, merchants and banks while replying to the questionnaires.

(8) The study focuses only on the post New Economic Policy era (after 1991). The Post 1991 era witnessed the tremendous growth of credit cards and credit card usage.

(9) The study pertains to the current trend prevailing on the whole and does not go in depth to the previous state of mind before the study or process of change that could have occurred.

(10) Considering availability of data, secondary data obtained has been on different years appearing sporadically.

CHAPTER SCHEME

Chapter I consists of Introduction, Scope of the Study, Objectives, Methodology, Hypotheses, Statistical tools employed in the course of the study to test these hypotheses and the Limitations of this study.

Chapter II deals with Review of Literatures pertaining to the study. It consists of the earlier studies made in this field. The books, journals and articles that had been reviewed for the better understanding of the study have been specified.

Chapter III analyzes the need to study the growth of credit card since it has seen a tremendous growth globally and its relative importance to India.

Chapter IV deals with the origin and growth of Credit Card System in India with particular reference to Chennai City and highlights the necessity of this study.

Chapter V deals with the analyses and interpretation of data collected. It centers on the issues on consumer behavior with reference to credit card possession at various income and education levels and the like. Also the pulse of the merchants who accept credit cards has been dealt with in detail. Banks' perception of issuing credit cards, their potentiality and their limits has also been dealt with, in this chapter.

Chapter VI summarizes the findings and tries to draw conclusions based on the entire study. Suggestions are given for the efficient functioning of Credit Card System in India.

NOTES

1. Ruddar Dutt and K.P.M. Sundharam (2006), 'Indian Economy', Rajendra Ravindra Printers (Pvt.) Ltd., Fifty Third Edition, New Delhi.
2. Ishwar C. Dingra (1995), "The Indian Economy–Resources, Planning, Development & Problems", Sultan Chand & Sons, New Delhi.
3. Jhingan M.L. (2006), "Monetary Economics", Vrinda Publications (P) Ltd., 6th edition, Delhi.
4. "Banking and Financial Systems", Sultan Chand & Sons, Educational Publishers, New Delhi, 1995.

5. Ishwar C. Dhingra (1995), "The Indian Economy", Sultan Chand & Sons, Educational Publishers, New Delhi.
6. Versatile Card Technology Brochure, 2005.
7. Jhingan M.L. (2006), "Monetary Economics", Vrinda Publications (P) Ltd., 6th edition, Delhi.
8. *www.ventureinfotek.com*
9. ICMA–Industry Information, 2004. *http://icma.com/info/training/history/history.asp*
10. Versatile Card Technology, information obtained from Sales & Marketing through discussion and interview by the researcher, , Chennai, 2007.
11. Kothari, C.R. (2005), "Research Methodology–Methods and Techniques", New Age International Publishers, Second Edition, New Delhi.

2

REVIEW OF LITERATURE

For attaining the background knowledge of the subject, it was essential to know the concept behind Payment Cards, its global importance and acceptance, the industry purview with respect to Asia, and the case of India in accordance to the rules and guidelines applicable to this particular sector. The following literatures were reviewed for the same to obtain better insight. These reviewed literatures include books newspapers and journals circulated around the globe with exclusivity to Payments Cards Industry (which discusses the global market), those pertaining to Asia, general consumer behavior analysis done by various economists, which has been reflected in the study, narrowing down to India with respect to papers on articles on globalization and liberalization, banking sector reforms and finally articles that have appeared in the local dailies and journals and views expressed about credit cards that had appeared on the internet. However, these reviews appear in alphabetical order within chronological order as follows:

Stigler has analyzed the work of Ernst Engel's (1857)[1] who studied the relationship between income and expenditure on different commodities. The law stated that, with given tastes or preferences, the proportion of income spent on food diminished as income increased. The law and findings of Engel had been a major breakthrough in the history of economics and economic theory since it analyzed the fact that as income increased the amount spent on inferior goods decreased.

Ando and Modigliani (1963)[2] had presented consumer behavior in a totally different angle wherein it had stated consumption to be a function of lifetime expected income of the consumer. Their analysis had laid the ground work for a fundamental revision of some of the theories regarding consumer and his consumption and his savings. The analysis showed the variation in the spending pattern of the consumer during his income earning period which changed in accordance to his expectation of the available resources.

James S. Duesenberry (1949)[3] presented consumer behavior which was not independent but interdependent instead. The analysis showed that individuals are more concerned with their consumption relative to other people's than they are with their absolute living standard; and that consumption relations are irreversible over time. The theory had been a major departure from other consumption theories and had stated that to 'keep up with the Joneses' in their consumption, the poor will spend a higher proportion of their income than the rich.

C.G. Gopalakrishna (1968)[4] has employed the method of principal components to analyze the variance among six variables, viz., (1) Expenditure on food, beverages and tobacco; (2) Expenditure on fuel and lighting; (3) Expenditure on clothing, bedding, foot-wear; (4) Expenditure on housing, household requisites and services; (5) Miscellaneous; and (6) Population.

C.V. Anuradha (1992)[5] has discussed in detail the impacts of NEP with respect to consumer behaviour and price variations. A detailed analysis of price change before and after the introduction of the NEP has been vividly described by her.

K.P. Malathi Shri, (1992)[6] has done a compare and contrast study of the Canara Bank's and Andhra Bank's credit cards used by the consumers, thereby bringing out the pros and cons of usage of the same. The dissertation ended with the note that Andhra Bank credit cards seemed to be superior due to its viable features.

L.Shankari, (1992)[7] has spoken about the introduction of credit card culture in the so called conservative city of Chennai (then known as Madras), and how this culture has fast caught up, much to the surprise of its prefixed title.

Mrs. K. Girija, (1992)[8] has studied how credit card has helped in the spending spree concept and thereby helping the consumers to have an increased purchasing power which otherwise would not have been possible if all payments were to be made by cash instantly.

Ishwar C. Dhingra (1995)[9] has discussed in detail the concept of New Economic Policy introduced in 1991, its impact on the various aspects like planning in India after NEP, its impact on the poor, NEP and inflation, agricultural investment, agricultural labor, globalization impact on various sectors in the Indian economy and the structural adjustment and technology invasion due to the NEP, which has provided a vivid and lucid picture of the NEP, 1991.

Agarwal Pradeep, Subir V Gokarn et al (1995)[10] have discussed the various policy reforms with reference to East Asia and India and analyzed the prospective of such reforms.

Kaushik Surendra K., (1995)[11] has analyzed the transformation of India into an emerging market after the NEP, 1991 with respect to the various economic reforms and financial reforms it had undertaken. A sharper view of the Indian economic system after the wake of NEP, 1991 has been undertaken in the study.

H.L. Ahuja (1998)[12] has discussed every aspect of Marshall's Diminishing Marginal Utility and its application in economic theory. A descriptive picture of Marshall's law stating that increase in the stock of a thing diminishes with every increase in the stock that a person already possess, has been entailed minutely.

Rupa Chanda (2002)[13] has focused her study on the various means and ends of globalization which furnishes in detail the various opportunities and challenges faced by India due to its policy of globalization and liberalization. The study has given a broader view with all its pros and cons.

Linda Punch (2004)[14] has analyzed the use of credit cards and falling into debt trap across many countries in a different, new angle. The study has shown that it was not just excessive use the sole reason for falling into bankruptcy but other factors like ill health, adverse litigation, gambling, unemployment, liabilities on guarantees etc., also contributed to debts. The study has focused on various vital issues worth noting by many developing countries which has high growth potential of credit cards.

Visa International, in conjunction with the Commonwealth Business Council (CBC) (2004)[15] has explored the social and economic benefits of electronic payments and has discussed in detail the benefits accrued by economies which have adopted electronic payments to assist economic growth and individual empowerment.

The paper has dealt exhaustively the value of electronic payment transactions which help to take friction out of an economy and more specifically the clear advantages of electronic payment systems over cash or paper-based systems, which could generate a number of significant, positive economic benefits. The paper has given a vivid picture as to the usage of credit cards leading to higher consumption and GDP since consumers holding credit cards tend to spend more. It has also cited suitable examples from countries across the globe with data and explanations which have adopted electronic payment systems and have gained a lot by way of increasing efficiency, improving financial transparency, technological development at a higher standard in hands with sophistication, efficiency in disbursements of payrolls, pensions and other benefits and reducing transactions costs by the banking sector. The paper has provided a major insight to the benefits and advantages of the electronic payment system wherein Credit Cards come under the head, 'account based electronic card', by sighting many examples of developed countries.

Arkadev Chatterjea, Robert Jarrow, Robert Neal and Yildiray Yildirim (2005)[16] have worked out a pricing model that banks can use to measure and manage the risks of their credit card operations. The model throws light on how valuable is credit card lending.

Dinamalar (2005)[17], a daily, has analyzed the advantages of co-branded credit petro cards for usage by the customers for fuelling their vehicles, in the regional language.

Manyara Kirago (2005)[18] has analyzed exclusively the vicious cycle of using credit cards and has thrown light on escaping this debt cycle. The analysis also throws light on the effective planning and wise usage of credit cards.

Darren Waggoner (2005)[19] has analyzed the specific case of U.S. youth holding credit cards, the implications and repercussions of the same.

Mark Beauchamp (2005)[20] has provided in his study, the need to know the various factors like profit potential, market size, competition, product implementation and service commitment before launching a new product. A deeper insight to these factors will help issuers of credit cards like banks in India, to get a better circulation of credit cards by their customers.

Mohan Sivanand (2005)[21] has highlighted in detail the different types of frauds that can be manipulated with a credit card and the facts that how many merchants do not even check the photo or verify the signature during purchases made by customers and with regard to banks' side, how irresponsible sometimes they are on reports of credit card theft or fraud. The article has been quite disheartening as the various factors highlighted makes someone to give a second thought before acquiring or using a credit card. This will ultimately prove to be a doom to the growth of credit card sector.

NCAER (2005)[22] (National Council of Applied Economic Research) has published a paper with a perspective on India – how individuals, businesses and the Government can benefit from a modern electronic payment network. It has identified new opportunities for payment innovation in government purchasing and procurement, government pension distribution, banking the unbanked, improving credit delivery for small businesses, facilitating inbound tourism and remittances among others. It was the first white paper of its kind on the Indian payment card industry. The paper has dealt in detail the banking reforms which came about after 1990. It has also analyzed in detail, given the experience of other emerging economies, how the adoption of a more modern, global and efficient payment system will help address some of the issues leading to greater transparency and efficiency as well as benefit consumers, retailers, the banking industry and the government. The paper has also described in detail the possibility in India to enhance government expenditure efficiency by reducing documentation and streamlining the administrative processes, reduce bureaucracy and the extent of losses due to slippage which occur due to under-utilization of productive capacity, lower human capital formation, inefficient allocation of resources and loss of revenue to the public exchequer that can be used for productive purposes. It has also viewed as to how International Card Payment Systems can provide alternative cost-effective channels for person-to-person remittances bringing more remittance funds within the formal economy as India is the world's largest remittance country and receives 15% of worldwide remittance flows.

The paper has also dealt in detail the launching of the Online Reservation with Payment Gateway System of TTDC on 02-07-2004 wherein by using credit cards, confirmation of bookings can be made instantly, thereby also encouraging tourism; increasing efficiency and lowering transactions cost of the current banking system through Electronic Payment System (EPS); by increasing the welfare of the people for a healthy economy through education, healthcare by means of EPS; cost effective way for the treasury to deliver refunds to taxpayers who have overpaid their tax through EPS are few examples that have been given importance in this paper.

Puja Mehra (2005)[23] has very carefully analyzed the booming credit card business in India along side the growing harassment in cases of defaulting customers. A new angle of restoring confidence has been clearly discussed.

Raghu Mohan (2005)[24] has studied the transformation the payment industry has been undergoing. The study has given a detailed account of perception from the banks' side and the credit card holders' side. A diverse angle of differential pricing due to cut throat competition has been dealt in the study which makes it important and worthy.

Richard Rolfe (2005)[25] has studied the banking sector reform in Turkey leading to growth in transactions through payment cards. The slow and steady growth of credit cards has been highlighted which gives a profound picture of banking sector reforms and credit card growth.

Richard Rolfe (2005)[26] has also analyzed the changes to the Russian tax code that had stimulated the growth of real revolving credit cards. The study has only focused the impediments that prevailed for the growth of payment card transactions and the change the economy has been undergoing which has a healthy sign in Russia.

Ved Prakash Gulati (2005)[27] has touched upon the different evolving payment systems in India while a mention has also been made on the rise of credit card payment via online and the risk of security has also been touched upon in the course of his article.

ABN Amro Bank (2006)[28] has analyzed the credit card business of the self highlighting banks which has been on the forefront of providing products packed with features and benefits customers could benefit. The study was exclusively based on UAE markets.

Prof. B. Appa Rao and K.B.D. Shobha Rani (2006)[29] have surfed on every aspect of consumer protection act under which lies the RBI Act, 1934. It is worth mentioning here that RBI has come out with banking ombudsman for Credit Card segment to resolve various issues connected to credit cards and credit card holders.

Damayanti Datta (2006)[30] has analyzed the judicious usage of credit cards alongside analyzing the credit card debts, which has come out with some promising views of certain heads of banks. The article concludes with two useful strong notes that credit card holders should never allow the card issuers to take them for granted, and never do anything that will make easy for the issuer to catch the credit card holder on the wrong side.

Gibson G. Vedamani (2006)[31] has analyzed consumerism and consumer behavior driving the retail sector in India. The growing middle class contributing to the rapid growth in consumption has been studied in detail. Also the Indian mentality of using the cash over credit cards and the changing scenario of younger generation has been very vividly handled in his analysis.

M.L. Jhingan (2006)[32] has studied Keynes' fundamental Psychological law of consumption function which presented consumption as a functional relationship, and the famous concept of propensity to consume and save gained importance. He wrote that '...men are disposed as a rule and on an average to increase their consumption as their income increases but not by as much as the increase in their income'. The analysis showed that the propensity to save depended on the income distribution and the relative consumption.

Joydeep Sengupta and Renny Thomas (2006)[33] have penetrated into the various aspects of consumers and their trade with banks for different issues. In short, a detailed account of what kind of services Indian consumers expect from banks has been elaborately discussed.

Mark Klammer (2006)[34] has done a spectacular study on payment card industry and globalization and the necessity to have knowledge on the local market since 'globalization' is a universal, wide-angled word. A specific reference to India wherein all players target just the top 2% of the population whereas greater potential lies in the unbanked population has been made, which, according to credit card sector in India, has been true. The article ends with the note of understanding specific market according to its customer with product differentiation.

Moinak Mitra (2006)[35] has discussed about the surfeit of airline co-branded credit cards today, each offering tempting advantages and discounts. The article has also discussed the lavish usage of credit cards without jumping into a debt trap by bringing in lot of redemption points, sometimes even for free air tickets.

Nivedita Mukherjee (2006)[36] has discussed the various issues on using credit cards and has discussed in detail the resolutions given by the RBI. The article highlights the importance of RBI Guidelines ruling credit cards and credit card holders.

Oommen A. Ninon (2006)[37] has discussed Banking Reforms in India and analyzed in detail the fact as to how the banking sector has to keep pace with the growing demands of its customers. He has dealt in detail the areas where focus has to be given in the banking sector, to improve its efficiency and competitiveness. Reform measures have also been entailed in detail in his analysis which included the beneficial impact of the reforms and the new challenges that has to be faced by this sector. The study has also analyzed the growth of retail banking and increasing role of technology in this sector. The study has made a major headway in the discussion of banking sector reforms in Indian banks.

Punam Mohandas (2006)[38] has enlightened in detail the many conveniences of possessing credit cards. However, the study has specific reference to UAE only.

A. Subramani (2006)[39] has entailed in detail the rights, duties and violations of credit card holders which throws light on the attentiveness and alertness to be maintained by plastic card users, especially the credit card users.

Sucheta Dalal (2006)[40], has discussed the various functions of banks dealing for a variety of reasons by people–from safekeeping their money to making payments either electronically or through credit and debit cards, or transacting in shares through depository accounts. Many banks even offer investment advice and portfolio management services. The article has been based on the first ever customer satisfaction survey of banks by a Delhi based NGO called VOICE. An exclusive insight by the survey has been made in this article, on various aspects of dealings with banks by customers. A spectacular review in totality of the banking services was done by the survey and some overwhelming findings with respect to credit cards has been found.

'The Hindu' (2006)[41] has given in its article, a detailed account of the 'Code of Bank's Commitment', given by RBI wherein details of protecting the cards by the cardholders, the do's and don'ts of cards have also been specified indetail.

Vietnam News (2006)[42] has highlighted in its article the waning of cash transactions with reference to Vietnam alone. The article has given a glimpse of the increasing use of card transactions.

Ananda Vikatan, (2007)[43] a magazine in the regional language, has touched upon details of various ways of latest credit card frauds in the words of police personnel, Mr. Murugan.

Deepika Khatri (2007)[44] has delved into the aspect of plastic money equaling buying power but also has analyzed the various factors hidden behind the credit card purchase. A glimpse of how to keep oneself away from debt trap and different ways to keep the card and its details safe has been elaborately done by her study.

Elda Christy (2007)[45] has enlisted in detail in her article the prudent use of credit cards. She has thrown light on the basic principles working on the credit card system. The study has given an essential understanding of the financial tool called the credit card.

Euromonitor International (2007)[46], a market research survey has dealt in detail the position of Financial Cards –India. It has been surveyed that Indian banks are getting aggressive by revamping themselves and gearing up to fight competition from the foreign players, especially by moving away from big cities to locales where access by foreign banks is quite low. With respect to credit card usage, it has reviewed the various aspects of the Indian Banking System, peoples' characteristic of "Buy now, pay now" which has been a major deterrent to the growth of credit card usage in the country. The survey has come out with some astonishing facts. Though the future of credit card penetration and usage has been predicted to be on the rise as credit card issuers focus on intensive marketing and advertising to entice card owners to spend with their cards, the general conclusion has been that card companies in India will take a much longer time to breakeven, approximately three years as compared to less than a year in Singapore. Also a possibility of card issuing companies with the combined functions of debit and credit might start issuing a single card, has been pointed out, as this would benefit the cardholders to have check on one card with minimal usage of plastic money.

Gini and Shankar (2007)[47] had entailed in their article, the various uses and advantages of possessing a credit card which comes quite handy like a friend in need during times of crisis like booking of tickets, unexpected hospital expenses, on-line transactions through credit cards without the fear of letting out the traditional method of letting out the details over telephone orally. They also have entailed in detail the necessity of careful handling of credit cards when handed over for swiping at various places like the petrol bunks, hotels and restaurants etc. which are areas prone to misuse and frauds, and frauds occurring on credit cards through outsourcing companies.

Kishore Biyani (2007)[48] has in his study analyzed in a sharper angle, the understanding of the different needs of the consumer. The study has highlighted the nation itself as a young nation and has categorized India and its consumers into two different types. In short, a broader perspective of the consumers in general has been considered, a totally different way of perceiving consumers.

A Merrill Lynch Survey (2007)[49] has viewed that India has grown rapidly in terms of cards issued though most Indians prefer to use a debit card. The research work has come out in detail the comparisons of various countries including India, in terms of Credit Cards Market, along with other aspects of its research.

M.V. Nair (2007)[50] in his study has highlighted the strategies and the emerging trends in the Indian Banking Industry. He has also highlighted the factors of globalization, liberalization, consumer aspects and technology which could bring about a change in the banking environment. He has analyzed the new angle perceived by the consumers towards banking contemplating with technology invasion. This analysis has thrown light on the new forces of globalization and liberalization, the twin forces, posing challenges. The study has in itself took a new dimension in the banking sector reforms of banks in India.

Nivedita Mukherjee with Rajesh Parishwad and Dyanesh Jathan (2007)[51], have given an overall view of the harassments and frauds made by credit card issuing banks on customers on various false grounds to the extent of making them suffer a literal stroke due to mental pressure and agony. Their article has given a detailed insight of the rosy picture being presented while issuing credit cards but the devil behind the veil. It has delved in detail the various hidden charges apart from service charges levied which appear only on the statements and not specified at the time of credit card issuance. Also the knack of sending the bills late deliberately by banks to levy late payment fee by various banks has also been brought to light which, of course, gives the darker side of possessing credit cards.

Tae Soo Kang and Guonan Ma (2007)[52] have given a vivid picture of several cycles of marked credit card booms and busts in Asia. The mechanics and the effects of the financial system and real economy has been brought to light in the various Asian countries of China, Singapore, Taiwan, Hong Kong, and Korea and the factors leading to the Credit card market booms and busts have been viewed and reviewed with a concluding note to policymakers to make use of the liberalization process.

Subha J. Rao (2007)[53] has given an exclusive picture of making a smart swipe with multiple credit cards too, without jumping into a debt trap. While intelligent usage of credit cards without defaulting has been discussed in her article, the intricacies underlying their usage has also been subtly specified which presents a worthy reading.

Sucheta Dalal (2007)[54], has given an insight about banking services which highlights the fact quite emphatically that menu of services and 24 x 7 ATM access alone need not build a relationship of trust. She has brought out the facts that how many private banks slap their customers by charging for "in-branch" transactions–something which can be treated as an extreme negative impact of customer satisfaction.

The article has also provided a detailed insight of debiting amount without explanations, hidden charges for negative consent, negotiation charges, hefty fees for existing credit card holders, the problem of offering credit card to a new credit card holder, charges levied on non usage of add-on cards which are supposed to be 'lifetime free', from all angles and has wound up by highlighting the necessity of knowing the various terms, conditions, other rules and regulations attached to a credit card by a cardholder.

Sucheta Dalal (2007)[55] again in her article has brought out the 'trailing interest' factor adopted by banks with special reference to U.S. and also has underlined the fact that 80% of complaints to RBI pertained to credit cards.

"Payment Card Industry Survey" (2001-2006)[56], surveys every year, the growth of the payment card industry and very meticulously and intricately brings out every detail of Credit Card Sector in India, like the number of issuers, their market share, their rankings, merchant establishments, their numbers and rankings, the growth of credit cards issuer-wise, key factors contributing to its growth, any obstacle faced by this segment etc. This yearly journal gives a thorough knowledge of credit card industry in India from all its directions.

The detailed study of relevant literature pertaining to the objectives of the thesis has helped the researcher to gather and analyze the data and test the hypotheses laid down.

NOTES

1. Stigler G. J., "The Early History of Empirical Studies of Consumer Behavior", *Journal of Political Economy*, Volume 62, No. 2.
2. Ando A. and Modigliani F. (1963), "The Life Cycle Hypothesis of Saving : Aggregate Implications and Tests", A.E.R., March.
3. James S. Duesenberry (1967), "Income, Saving and the Theory of Consumer Behaviour", Harrard University Press, Cambridge, Manchester.
4. Gopalakrishna, C. G. (1968), "Ranking of Cities according to Costliness", *The Indian Economic Journal*, Vol. XV, No. 5, April-June.
5. Anuradha, C. V. (1992), "Price Variations and Consumer Behaviour Before and After New Economic Policy–1991", unpublished M.Phil, Dissertation.
6. Malathi Shri K. P. (1992), "A study on Credit Card System: A comparative study with special reference to Andhra Bank and Canara Bank, unpublished M.Phil., dissertation.
7. L. Shankari (1992), "Bank Credit Card Culture in Madras City,"unpublished M.Phil. Dissertation, November.
8. Mrs. K. Girija (1992), "A Study on the Impact of Credit Cards on the Purchasing Power of Cardholders", Unpublished M.Phil., dissertation.

9. Ishwar C. Dhingra (1995), "The Indian Economy–Resources, Planning, Development and Problems", Sultan Chand and Sons, New Delhi.

10. Agarwal, Pradeep, Subir V. Gokarn, Veena Mishra, Kirti S. Parikh and Kunal Sen (1995), "Economic Restructuring in East Asia and India : Prospectives on Policy Reforms, IGNOU, Working Paper.

11. Kaushik, Surendra K. (1995), "India's Economic and Financial Reforms and Its Transformation into an Emerging Market", Institute of Economic Growth, Working Paper 174.

12. Ahuja, H. L. (1998), "Modern Economics", S. Chand & Company Ltd., New Delhi, Eighth revised edition.

13. Rupa Chanda (2002), "Globalization of Services: India's Opportunities and Constraints, Oxford University Press, New Delhi.

14. Linda Punch (2004), "Going Abroad: Bad Debt", Credit Card Management, Thomson Media Publications, New York, Vol. 17, No. 4, July, pp. 38-41.

15. Commonwealth Banking and Financial Services Conference, "Payment Solutions for Modernizing Economies", Commonwealth Business Council and Visa, Published White Paper, September, 2004.

16. Arkadev Chatterjea, Robert Jarrow, Robert Neal and Yildiray Yildirim (2005), *The Journal of Derivatives*, winter 2003, Indian Brand Equity Foundation, Gurgaon, February. *www.ibef.com*

17. Dinamalar (2005), "Credit Card, Debit Card, ATM Card", Dinamalar Publications, Chennai, November 13.

18. Manyara Kirago (2005), "Escaping the Debt Cycle", Your Money-*Times of India Publication*, Mumbai, October 9–November 4.

19. Darren Waggoner (2005), "Youth + Cards = Debt", Cards and Payments–Credit, Debit and Beyand, Source Media Publications, Vol. 1, No. 1, Illinois, June.

20. Marc Beauchamp (2005), "What you need to know before launching a new product", *Transaction World Magazine*, Vol. 1, Issue 5, U.S., January.

21. Mohan Sivanand (2005), "How Safe in Your Credit Card", Reader's Digest, Living Media Publications Limited, Chennai, May.

22. National Council of Applied Economic Research, "Development of Electronic Payment Systems in India", A Published Paper, Visa International Asia Pacific Banks' Association and NCEAR, January 2005.
23. Puja Mehra (2005), "Restoring Credit", India Today, Living Media Publications Ltd., Chennai, July 25.
24. Raghu Mohan (2005), Business India, Raheja Group of Publications, Mumbai, January 17-30.
25. Richard Rolfe (2005), "Carving up Turkey", European Card Review, ECR Publishing Partnership LLP, Vol. 12, No.5, September/October , pp. 18-20.
26. Richard Rolfe (2005), "Russian Revolution", European Card Review, ECR Publishing Partnership LLP, Vol. 12, No.6, November/December.
27. Ved Prakash Gulati (2005), "Indian Payment Systems a Revolution in the Offing", *Electronics Today,* Vol. 38, No.2, Meenathethil Printers, Mumbai, September.
28. Abn Amro (2006), "Value for Your Money", *Khaleej Times,* UAE, September 20.
29. Prof. Appa Rao B. and Shobha Rani K.B.D. "Consumer Protection Act: Application to Banking Service", *Indian Banker,* Volume 1, No. 1, January 2006.
30. Damayanti Data (2006), "Plastic Promise", *India Today,* Living Media Publications Limited, Chennai, March 27.
31. Gibson G. Vedamani (2006), "A Revolution in the Making", *The Hindu* Survey of Indian Industry, The Hindu Group of Publications, Chennai, pp. 258-260.
32. Jhingan M. L. (2006), "The Economics of Development and Planning", Vrinda Publications (P) Ltd. New Delhi, 38th revised edition.
33. Joydeep Sengupta and Renny Thomas (2006), *India Today,* Living Media Publications Limited, Chennai, Feb. 27.
34. Mark Klammer (2006), "The Importance of Local Knowledge in a Globalised Economy", Cards Now! Asia, Jeera-Ju Media Group Sdn Bhd, Malaysia, Vol. 7, No.1, January/February.
35. MOINAK MITRA, "Plastic Money", Outlook Money, Outlook Publishing (India) Pvt. Ltd., Chennai, June 15, 2006.

36. Nivedita Mukherjee (2006), "Card-inal Issues", The Week, Malayala Manorama Publications, Kottayam, January 8.

37. Oommen A. Ninon (2006), "Keeping pace with demands", *The Hindu Survey of Indian Industry*, The Hindu Group of Publications, Chennai, pp. 49-52.

38. Punam Mohandas (2006), "Plastic Money and Its Many Conveniences", *Khaleej Times*, September 20.

39. A. Subramani (2006), *The Hindu*, The Hindu Group of Publications, Chennai, November 16.

40. Sucheta Dalal (2006), "How Good Is Your Bank", Money Life, Moneywise Media Publications Pvt. Ltd., Mumbai, Volume 1, Issue 15, Chennai.

41. *"The Hindu"*, The Hindu Group of Publications, Chennai, July 14, 2006.

42. *Vietnam News*, "Cash Transactions on the Wane", The National English Language Daily, Vietnam, January 13, 2006.

43. Ananda Vikatan (2007), Vasan Publications (P) Limited, Chennai, August 1.

44. Deepika Khatri (2007), "Counting the Credit", *India Today*, Woman Living Media Publications Limited, Kancheepuram, August.

45. Elda Christy (2007), "Check Your Credit Card's 'Interest Free Period' Before You Swipe It", *Times of India* Publication, Mumbai, March 20.

46. Euromonitor International Survey: Country Market Insight, "Financial Cards: India", A Published Paper, March 2007.

47. Gini and Shankar (2007), "Puli Vaalai Piditha Kathai", (Meaning the Repercussions on Holding the a Tail of a Tiger, Here the Tiger Referring to Credit Cards), Kungumam, Kungumam Group of Publications, Chennai, 17th May.

48. Kishore Biyani (2007), "Lure of huge consumer base", Hindu Survey of Indian Industry, The Hindu Group of Publications, Chennai.

49. Merrill Lynch Survey Report (2007), "Banking in the BRICs", a Published Market Research Survey, 28 February.

50. M.V. Nair (2007), "Banking : Exciting growth avenues", *The Hindu* Survey of Indian Industry, The Hindu Group of Publications, Chennai, pp. 49–52.

51. Nivedita Mukherjee (2007), with Rajesh Parishwad and Dyanesh Jathan, "Credit Card Trap", The Week, Malayala Manorama Publications, Kottayam, June 17.

52. Tae Soo Kang and Guonan Ma (2007), "Recent Episodes of Credit Card Distress in Asia", *BIS Quarterly Review*, a Published Paper, June.

53. Subha J. Rao (2007), "Make a Smart Swipe", *The Hindu Metro Plus*, The Hindu Group of Publications, Chennai, September 17.

54. Sucheta Dalal (2007), "Get Your Banking Problems Resolved", *Money Life–Personal Magazine*, Volume 2, Issue 13, Moneywise Media Pvt. Ltd., Mumbai, August 30.

55. Sucheta Dalal (2007), "Watch that Credit Card Spend", Money Life, Moneywise Media Publications Pvt. Ltd., Mumbai, Vol. 2, Issue 14, September 14.

56. Indian Payment Card Industry, "Venture Infotek Research Publication", 2001–2006, *www.ventureinfotek.com*

3

AN OVERVIEW OF THE GLOBALCREDIT CARD SYSTEM

Credit Card Sector has taken a huge leap, just not in India alone, but all over the world. The famous Plastic Money has taken the world in its stride. Hence it becomes not only necessary but also important to study the need for this particular sector. In order to know the same, it becomes inevitable to study the origin and growth of this sector, globally in general, and in India, in particular. In this chapter, the researcher has studied in brief, the various types of credit cards, its uses in general to different factors involved in a credit card transaction, a synopsis of its mechanism and the global scenario. In order to gain better knowledge of the study, the scope of credit card industry and its immensity in growth has also been touched upon because the transformation from paper-based currency to plastic based has already been deep-rooted in developed countries. However, its entry to developing countries like India has been just two decades ago which is multi cultured, linguistic, and co-existence of 'reservation' and 'conservatism' alongside 'cosmopolitism' being present. Though the culture of using plastic currency started late, it has caught up quickly like forest fire. With globalization taking its course in every aspect around the world, India too has got itself attached to this process. Belonging to part of the globe, usage of credit cards in India automatically attaches itself in the global usage figures. Hence, the scope of this industry, too, has been touched upon, in brief.

TYPES OF CREDIT CARDS

There are three basic types of Credit Cards which are as follows. First being the travel and entertainment cards such as American Express or Diners Club. They have no predetermined spending limits and must be paid in full each month. Second are the bank cards such as MasterCard, Visa, Discover, Optima, GM and Ford cards which are sponsored by individual banks. The bank defines spending limit (sometimes called credit lines) and each offers different terms and conditions. The third type belongs to the house cards that are good only in one chain of stores, such as Spears, J.C.Penny, Shell, or Mobil. These cards are only accepted by the specific company and so do not have an annual fee. However, the terms and conditions of these cards vary widely. Apart from this we have what we call as the affinity card, typically a MasterCard or Visa– carries the logo of an organization in addition to the lender's emblem.

AUTHENTICATION OF CREDIT CARD TRANSACTION

Three basic methods of Credit Card Authentication are: Voice Authorization, Electronic Data Capture (EDC) or Point of Sale (POS) terminals and Virtual Terminals from the Internet.

Normally for authorization, transaction validity and record on the Glossary is checked. For usage on ATM, PIN is required to be used. When the acquirer company gets the Credit Card authentication request, it checks the transaction for validity and the record on the Mag stripe for Merchant ID, Valid Card Number, Expiration date, Credit Card Limit and Card Usage. Once this has been established, the transaction itself is carried out in encrypted form.

USERS OF A CREDIT CARD

(1) Credit Card Holder

(2) Merchant/Services Provider

(3) Transactions Acquiring Bank (sometimes the issuing bank itself can be the acquiring bank)

(4) Association (VISA/MASTERCARD etc.)

(5) Credit Card Issuing Bank.

BENEFITS OF CREDIT CARDS

Due to a credit card transaction, all the above mentioned people stand to be benefited by one way or the other. The benefits are discussed in brief by each party which are as follows:

Card Holders

It gives easy availability of Revolving Credit Facility which could not be provided even by debit cards. By revolving credit facility is meant that by making a payment for the bill generated due to swiping a credit card for a month, the consumer is asked to pay only a certain minimum amount of the bill and not the full payment. The balance amount could be carried over for the next installment, but with interest rate charged on it.

Apart from the above, it provides an inbuilt credit limit for transit period at no extra cost. It gives cash withdrawal facilities from Automated Teller Machines (ATMs). Consumers need not depend on the banks and their timings for withdrawal of cash. ATMs function 24 hours a day and a consumer can withdraw money to a certain fixed amount from any of the ATMs of his choice or convenience or location in a day. Hence he is facilitated with tension-free timings of withdrawing his money which basically no bank could provide. Also these ATMs function on national holidays or holidays declared due to specific reasons that might occur unexpectedly. One cannot foresee such other unexpected holidays and the holding of credit cards come handy during such crisis.

Additional facilities like insurance, discounts, and privileges from time to time are also being provided to the consumers for wooing the customers to use their bank credit card. Such privileges do not come under other debit or ATM cards. Convenience of extra purchasing power without the hassle of carrying cash contributes to the main factor of the importance of credit card. Though a debit card may also be attributed to the similar feature, a credit card holding does not require the consumer to have a bank balance or a pre fixed amount in the bank as the case may be for debit cards. As the name suggests it gives the credit facility to the individual and hence even without a pre fixed amount, one can swipe the card and arrange for payments on a later date as suggested by the generation of the statement bill.

Delegating expending power to 'add-on' members like spouse, children etc., is also an added advantage of holding a credit card. Without applying for a fresh credit card, the prime credit card holder can acquire such add on cards for their spouse and children. And the latter need not be an earning member as far as the prime credit cardholder is able to make the payments swiped by these add-on cards. Thus reliance only on the prime credit card holder by other family members could be ruled out and during times of emergency, they could always use their card. Last but not least, a credit card helps in times of urgency. This is so when we do not expect certain expenditures or carry cash expecting such expenditures. Since it helps us in making instant decisions due to its possession, it is quite helpful, for the good or the service which would be available then may not be available later when we arrange for cash or arrange for depositing certain amount in the bank to use the debit card.

Merchants

As far as the benefits to merchants are concerned accepting a credit card would mean promoting sales due to the increased purchasing power of cardholder. Since the cardholder now need not worry about the price or the amount which he has carried, it boosts sales of the merchants on accepting it. Also, unlike debit cards, even if the price of a commodity which a credit cardholder feels worthy, of high utility value, he could purchase the same from the merchant even if his bank balance does not show a rosy picture. As long as the issuing bank shows the safe credit limit on his account, a merchant is safe of the sales made by the customer. Hence he need not lose the customer due to shortage of cash or bank balance (required for debit card).

Moreover, unlike earlier times before the introduction of the electronic data coding system, now due to advanced technology adopted in India as in the rest of the world, which has been adopted contributed by the globalization policy more so after NEP 1991, there is better liquidity due to quick realization of sale proceeds. The moment a credit card is swiped, the merchant knows whether the transaction could be proceeded or not since the very next second he gets information of his safe balance. If not, the transaction need not take place at all since the customer can adopt an alternate mode of payment, which could again be another credit card in case he holds multiple cards.

Also, a merchant gets additional credit facilities from the acquiring bank, free publicity in merchant directory and preferred for purchases by cardholder, thus increasing the clientele base.

Banks

Benefits accrued by banks by issuing their bank's credit cards are also multifarious. Initially to quote, it improves bank's image. When a customer acquires a bank's credit card to have in his wallet, in general, he feels secure with the bank he transacts. This message is easily reached by the bank to the customer. This will further be supported the more and more he swipes the bank card. This improves the image amidst the merchants too, thereby increasing acceptability. The more a credit card is swiped for various purposes, the lesser the paper and coin based transaction, lesser time by the bank authorities to regulate cash based operation, more efficient working system contributing to the development of the economy since in many developing countries like India, banks form the backbone to development. Also, clear picture of the expenses made by its customers known which means a clear taxation policy that could be adopted by the economy knowing the expending pulse of the people. In India, it has been found that many are spending more than they earn and the amount derived for such expenditures are unaccounted. This can be averted by use of credit cards.

Apart from the above, credit card segment shows a profitable business for banks. It also forms an additional avenue to acquire new customers. It facilitates retention of existing accounts and canvassing of new accounts. The banks also benefit through funding purchases/withdrawals in foreign currencies leading to exchange profit. Exchange profit also helps the economy directly and lastly there is additional channel for funds utilization.

Associations of Credit Cards (Visa/Master/AMEX/Others)

Without leaving the associations or institutions authorizing the credit cards in its stride, credit cards benefit them too by increasing the member base – MasterCard issues shares in Capital to banks. Also, there is franchise fees earnings, income through transaction processing fees and brand image building, to mention a few.

Earning in Credit Card Business

On every transaction done through a credit card, the acquiring bank, the association and the card issuing bank earn income.

The merchant gives a discount of certain percentage of the transaction value; usually say 2% of which the card issuing Bank gets 1.1%[1]. Hence the Credit Card business is lucrative when the number of cards and the number of transactions are large.

In addition to the above, the card issuing banks normally charge fees/charges for different transactions/services like joining fee, annual fee, add on joining fee, add on annual fee, card replacement fee, PIN generation fee, late payment fee, over limit fee, renewal fee, cheque bounce fee, limit enhancement fee, ATM usage fee, cash advance fee and service charges, calculated like interest for the period availed, like cash advance charges and revolving credit charges.

Figure 1 shows the mechanism of a credit card transaction. To explain in brief, once a credit card transaction is produced to a merchant by a customer for swiping, on one hand, the merchant immediately checks for its validity and fund availability which in turn is checked with the acquirer bank. If these processes are through, the product or service

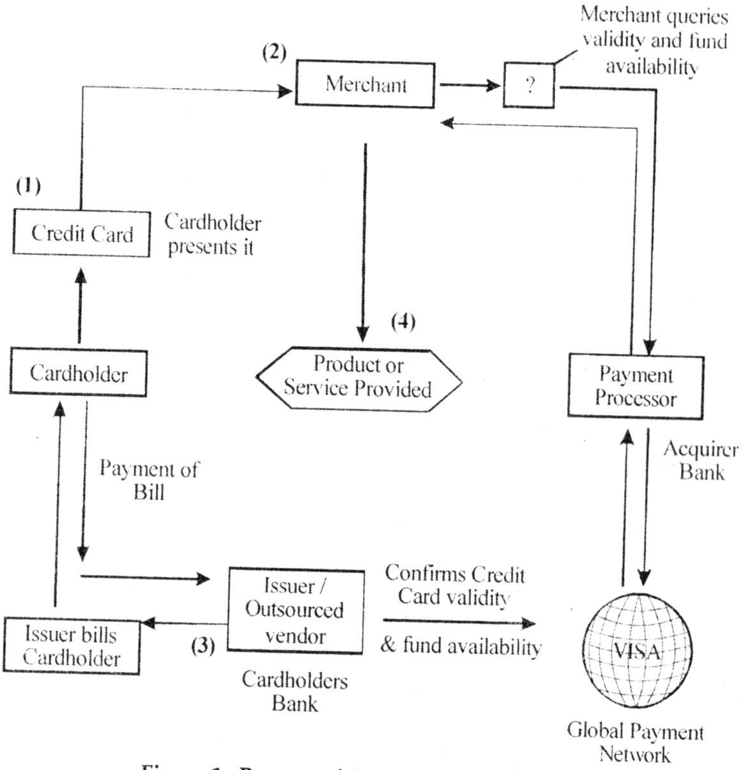

Figure 1 : Process of Credit Card Mechanism

is immediately provided to the consumer. On the other hand, the consumer receives a bill after a lapse of specified time limit from the bank confirming the purchase (in case of huge amount, sometimes, an immediate intimation is given to the consumer on his mobile, the moment the process is through, by certain banks), credit validity and balance availability. Thus the cycle follows for every credit card transaction done.

GLOBAL SCENARIO

Now, with the basic understanding of the Credit Card system, let us look at the two fundamental and unique card markets in existence today.

Plastic cards are arranged in two groups:

Secure Cards

Some of the primary kinds of secure cards issued are–

(a) Credit Card
(b) Debit Card
(c) ATM Card
(d) Financial Card
(e) Non Financial Cards like government cards and health cards.

Non-Secure or Standard Cards include

(a) Loyalty Cards
(b) Identification Cards
(c) Access Control Cards
(d) Gift Cards
(e) Promotional Cards
(f) Vending Cards
(g) Membership Cards
(h) Transportation Cards.

CREDIT CARDS come under the head 'Secure Cards'. It is a type of retail transaction settlement and credit system, named after the small plastic card issued to users of the system. The credit card issuer lends the consumer money and it allows the consumer to 'revolve' his balance, at the cost of having interest charged. Most credit cards are the same shape and size, as specified by the ISO 7810 Standards.

In order to cover all aspects of a credit card and for better understanding, a general overview of the industry scope and its immensity has been browsed upon.

INDUSTRY SCOPE

In 1999, the plastic card industry produced 7.9 billion cards, for a total of 4.5 billion dollars globally. In 2000, the industry produced 8.8 billion cards for a total of 4.3 billion dollars globally.

Cards also help leverage programs, products, convenience and commerce especially in the fields of finance, health care and communications. The influence of plastic cards extends much further as it continues to stimulate growth in other numerous areas such as identification, membership, transportation and mobile commerce leading the list. Companies use plastic cards to build relationships, promote corporate and product image, and create added convenience to transactions.

IMMENSITY OF THE PLASTIC CARD MARKET

The table below gives a global overview extracted from a survey sponsored by ICMA for the year 2000.

Table 1
Global Cards Manufactured for the Year 2000

Type	*Millions of Cards*	*Millions of U.S. Dollars*
Non Secure Cards	3498	402
Chip Cards	1603	3236
Other Secure Cards	1567	230
Other Financial Cards	1058	173

Source: The Voice of the Plastic Card Industry, "ICMA–Industry Information", 2000. *http://icma.com/info/training/history/history.asp*

Table 1 shows the different types of cards manufactured globally in the year 2000. As stated earlier, credit cards come under the head 'secure cards' and from table 1, it can be seen that 1567 millions of secure cards were produced for a value of 230 million US dollars.

Table 2 shows the region-wise production of cards produced around the world. North America includes Canada and the USA. It forms the most matured and developed market for cards followed by Europe. Since Asia-Pacific is considered to be a developing market, there is still scope for Asia-Pacific region to touch the level of matured markets of North America and Europe. In the Asian-Pacific region, Singapore, Taiwan, Malaysia and Hong Kong had already made a head start in the cards sector. The next target regions for the institutions, issuers and operators of credit cards are India and China, both showing tremendous potential. As for the case of India, there is a congenial atmosphere and free air for the system to flourish, enhanced especially after the introduction of NEP in 1991, where lot of liberalization and privatization has given way for various sectors to function independently. Joining hands with globalization, India can march ahead of other Asian countries, with proper understanding and functioning of the system. As of 2005, there were over 3.5 million merchants and 417 million cardholders worldwide. There were more than 1400 card issuers of card processing.[2]

Table 2
Global Market Share for the Year 2000

(in Millions)

Region	*Total Units*
North America*	4637.1
Europe	2149.8
Asia-Pacific	1460.7
Latin America	541.3
Middle-East/Africa	107.2
*includes Canada and the USA	

Source: The Voice of the Plastic Card Industry, "ICMA–Industry Information", 2004. *http://icma.com/info/training/history/history.asp*

Banking Cards

This is the second biggest market with 2004 shipments projected at 275 million units. The bank sector was predicted to rise by 21% in the next few years, i.e., by 2005-2006. Today, bank cards is a fast growing business. It is largely dependent on state-of-the-art technology. At the outset, the card business is a vital core business for banks, the flagship of retail products and in some cases, it represents large chunk of their profits. It is also a relationship that has to do with "customer's money".

Thus, with growing bank cards, aggressive card marketing is taking place towards a group being described as the "new affluent". Fairly typically, the affluent tend to spend higher amounts on their credit cards and default less than the typical customer, making them extremely attractive to credit card companies.

It would be worth noting here that in India (belonging to South Asia as per the world map), it is only the banks which are issuing credit cards unlike other countries wherein Non Governmental Organizations (NGOs) and other types of operators are also in the field in producing cards. Such being the condition and with the vision that banking cards being the second biggest market, India seem to have a lot of scope in improving its economy by adopting the payment system in general and credit card system in particular in various segments.

GROWTH BY SECTOR IN VARIOUS COUNTRIES

Monitoring the distribution of financial cards for the period 1999-2004, debit cards saw strong growth followed by credit cards. In major developed markets, such as Australia and the UK, credit cards saw growth driven by aggressive marketing and promotional activity. There was tremendous growth potential of emerging markets such as China and Russia. Nevertheless, the growing popularity of debit cards acted as a significant constraint on the development of credit cards, particularly in the debt-reluctant markets like India.

Table 3
Global Distribution of Cards for The Year 2004

Type of Card	*Percentage*
Debit Cards	50.8
Credit Cards	24.2
ATM Cards	11.6
Charge Cards	10.3
Store Cards	2.9
E-purse Cards	0.1

Source: Financial Cards–World, "Euromonitor International", 2004.

Table 3 shows that next only to debit cards, credit card segment hold the second largest share in the world with 24.2%. However, the figure of credit card sector showing a lesser percentage to debit cards could be due to the bias of income distribution found in many developing countries like India where a very small percentage are very well off with a drastic contrast of poverty equally ruling the roost on the other side sandwiched by the middle income group who are just rising in life only from the current generation and hence people are debt reluctant. Also another reason could be that many developed countries have started reaching a saturation point in credit cards. Yet another important factor could also be that

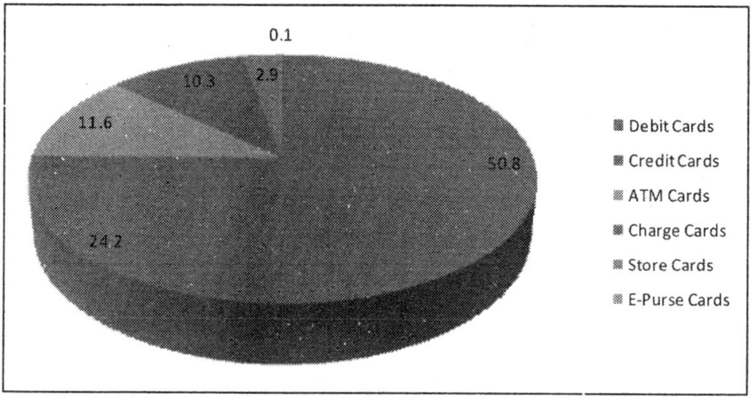

Figure 2 : Sectoral Distribution (in percentage)

many countries are yet to be tapped for their potential in the field of credit cards. The sectoral distribution as shown in the table can be shown in the pie diagram 2 as follows.

However, with globalization being the 'mantra' to various countries, the world has now shrunken barring many types of barriers. With due impart of education which automatically leads to expansion, import of knowledge, the root of technology, the vision of credit cards taking over debit cards the world over may not be too far.

Some of the biggest card figures of all are expected from India and China (Asia-Pacific Region). Around the globe, countries' move to card-based payments is rapid.

By end 2007, Italy will be the only European market where credit card use overweighs debit cards. Currently, Italy has many functions from arranging travel and holidays to helping to organize birthday presents, card protection service, travel insurance etc. to its esteemed cardholders.

US also have shifted its paradigm from the regular cash and cheque based payments to electronic payments of late. This s obvious from the figure 3.

1995

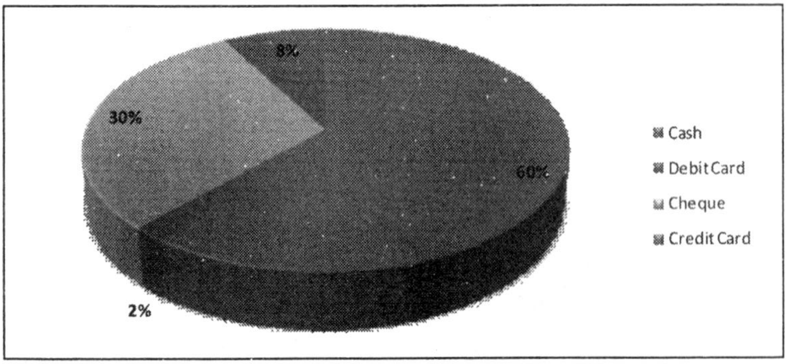

2003

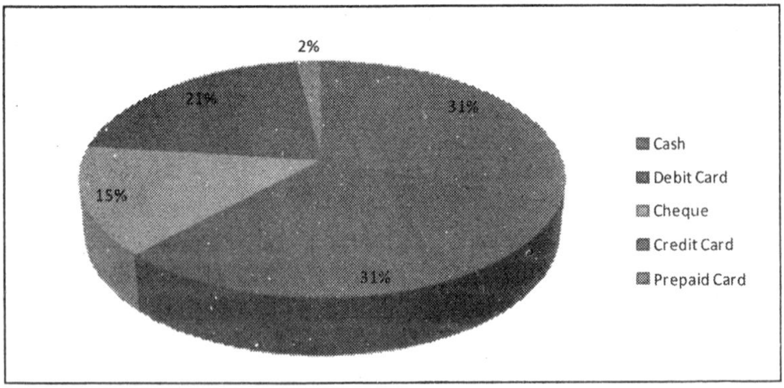

Source: Tower Group, Fortune 2004.

Figure 3 : Share of credit cards in 1995 and 2003.

the third highest number of credit cards in circulation in European Union (EU), behind Spain and the U.K., according to research consultancy, Mintel. Kalia card in Italy provides

Figure 3 shows how the US consumers' payment methods have drastically changed from cash and cheque based payments to electronic payment methods. It also shows that usage of credit cards have risen from a mere 8% in 1995 to 21% in 2003[1]. This shows the importance of growing credit card system. It can also be contrived from the figure 3.3 that as economic reforms take place around the globe, paper and coin based systems are getting lesser importance contemplated by the importance of plastic money. Economically speaking, plastic money can undergo more number of circulations than paper money. This saves time and production cost for any economy, the savings of such could be put to use for better utilization of resources in developing the economy in question. Better utilization of resources, needless to say, is the path to development. More the development, the better will be equitable distribution of goods and services to the people and lesser would be the inequality. And this being the main aim for any country in the world, plastic money provides a better solution.

Apart from Italy and US, another matured market is Taiwan. Now the credit card players have begun to target younger consumers in this country.

Switzerland is yet another country which has gone a long way in usage of credit cards. PAY & GO, a pioneering concept combines both a credit card and a ticket to book events by phone or online in Switzerland. This card is recognized as a valid ticket.

Turkey, too, has shown tremendous growth in bank credit cards in the past few years. This can be validated by the following Table 4, which shows only an increasing trend of credit card growth per cent.

Table 4 shows the percentage growth of credit cards in Turkey till 2004 which has been steadily increasing from 13,408 millions to 26,681 millions. Also a competition between the major issuers of Visa and MasterCard to increase their market share could be witnessed. Hong Kong and Shanghai Banking Corporation (HSBC) has found a huge potential in Turkey, targeting 30,000 cardholders by the year 2010.

Table 4
Percentage Growth of Credit Cards in Turkey-2004

(in Millions)

Issuers/ Year	*Visa*	*% Increase**	*Master Card*	*% Increase**	*Private Label*	*% Increase**	*Total*
1	*2*	*3*	*4*	*5*	*6*	*7*	*2+4+6*
2000	8281	61.8	5069	37.8	59	0.4	13408
2001	7830	55.9	6102	43.6	65	0.5	13997
2002	7947	50.6	7718	49.1	40	0.3	15705
2003	9572	48.2	10256	51.6	35	0.2	19863
2004	13202	49.5	13451	50.4	28	0.1	26681

Source: BKM, Survey, "European Card Review", 2005.
*calculated by the researcher.

Many European Countries tend to have an interest in reducing cash use so as to cut the size of black money. This is evident from Table 5 which shows the usage of more cards leading to a reduction in black money circulation in general.

Table 5
Performance of Cards and Black Money in Europe 2003

	Size as % of GDP		
Country	*Average 2001-2002*	*Average 2002-2003*	*Increase/ Decrease **
Austria	10.6	10.8	+0.2
Belgium	22.0	21.5	-0.5
Denmark	17.9	17.5	-0.4
Finland	18.0	17.6	-0.4
France	15.0	14.8	-0.2
Germany	16.3	16.8	+0.5
Greece	28.5	28.3	-0.2
Netherlands	13.0	12.8	-0.2
Norway	19.0	18.7	-0.3
Italy	27.0	26.2	-0.8
Portugal	22.5	22.3	-0.2
Spain	22.5	22.3	-0.2
Sweden	19.1	18.7	-0.4
Switzerland	9.4	9.5	+0.1
U.K.	12.5	12.3	-0.2
Ireland	15.7	15.5	-0.2

Source: Schneider (2005), European Card Review, 2006.
* computed by the researcher

In Table 5, plus (+) sign indicate an increase in black money while a minus (-) sign indicate a reduction in black money of the country in question. Table 5 shows that almost all countries except Austria, Germany and Switzerland have shown a decline in black money due to increase in payment card transactions. Though the decline has been marginal, it has been a welcoming feature since more transparency could be obtained and usage of cards has been one of the contributors to this positive feature.

Table 6
Country-wise Value of Credit Cards

(in US Dollars)

Country/ Year	*1999*	*2000*	*2001*	*2002*	*2003*	*%2004 World Total*	*No. of Times the Growth in 2003**
Canada	115.7	121.5	120.4	123.3	148.3	6.5	1.3
	(18.4)	(19.3)	(19.1)	(19.6)	(23.6)		
Brazil	22.9	27.5	24.7	22.6	26.6	1.2	1.2
	(18.4)	(22.1)	(19.9)	(18.2)	(21.4)		
Hong Kong,	14.7	18.2	20.9	21.6	21.8	1.0	1.5
China	(15.1)	(18.7)	(21.5)	(28.2)	(22.4)		
South Africa	7.5	8.1	7.6	7.2	11.9	0.6	1.6
	(17.7)	(19.1)	(18.0)	(17.0)	(28.1)		
Mexico	6.4	7.7	9.4	13.2	13.0	0.5	2.0
	(12.9)	(15.5)	(18.9)	(26.0)	(26.2)		
Portugal	6.4	7.1	7.1	8.6	11.0	0.5	2.0
	(15.9)	(17.7)	(17.7)	(21.4)	(27.4)		
Sweden	1.6	1.8	1.8	1.9	2.2	0.1	1.4
	(17.2)	(19.4)	(19.4)	(20.4)	(23.7)		
France	0.8	0.8	0.8	0.9	1.2	0.0	1.5
	(17.8)	(17.8)	(17.8)	(20.0)	(26.7)		
Russia	0.0	0.0	0.0	0.1	0.5	0.1	5.0
	–	–	–	(16.7)	(83.33)		
Australia	38.3	43.8	47.1	69.7	84.1	4.7	2.2
	(13.5)	(15.5)	(16.6)	(24.6)	(29.7)		

Source: Financial Cards: World, "Euromonitor International", 2004.

Figures within brackets and *computed by the researcher. It shows the percentage growth of a particular year to the total, approximating to the nearest tens after the first decimal point.

Table 6 shows the value of credit cards in US dollars for the years 1999-2004 produced country-wise. The table includes developed credit card markets such as Mexico and Australia, developing markets such as Hong Kong, South Africa and markets with bright future like Russia. It is also clear from the table that in all the countries, the percentage increase (shown within brackets) from 1999 to 2003 has been phenomenal. All countries have shown only a positive relationship. Russia too, from 16.7% in 2002 has shown five times growth in 2003 with 83.3%. Developed markets include Mexico and Australia. It is worth noting here that, in general, black economy, red tapism, corruption, bribery etc. are quite low in Australia when compared to other countries of the world. Also inequality of incomes is also quite low when compared to its population with the rest of the individual country's population. All these factors could have contributed to the fast and vast development of usage of credit cards in Australia which is shown by 29.7% growth in 2003 when compared to 13.5% in 1999. Mexico, belonging to United States, has been one among the firsts to adopt globalization and reap the fruits of it. Here too, the value of credit cards usage has shown a high percentage growth of 26.2% in 2003 when compared to 1993 (12.9%), twice the growth during this period.

Other countries too like the fast developing countries of Hong Kong, South Africa, France etc. are following suit. Russia's growth in the value of credit cards has been amazing within a span of one year. Several of the world's major credit cards markets saw a favorable economic climate spur growth in credit card value towards the end of 2004. The favourable economic climate encouraged a shift in the perception of credit cards in several markets. US alone accounted for nearly 56% of the global sector value. Operators worked to extend their networks and embed credit cards in the day-to-day financial activities. China appears to be an attractive emerging market for operators and issuers.

Table 7 shows the country wise per capita value transactions distribution through credit cards through the years 1999 to 2004 by several countries. Developed markets dominate the table of per capita credit card performance. High levels of credit card spending in markets are underpinned by high levels of personal disposable income and extremely well developed banking and telecommunication infrastructures. The researcher, however, has tried to calculate the increase or decrease in the percentage growth of per capita value of credit card transactions in the countries as mentioned in table 7. Once again, Australia has stood apart with a rise of 29.9% increase in 2004 when compared to 9.4% in 1999, 3.2 times the growth for the same period. However, Malaysia, which is an Asia-Pacific region has seen a tremendous growth rate of 31.4% in 2004 when compared to 12.1% in 1999 followed by Portugal with 25% (twice the increase in 2004 when compared to 1999) and then by Taiwan with the growth rate of 25.4% in 2004. As already discussed earlier, Taiwan is a matured market with respect to credit card sector. Venezuela showed a decreasing trend with respect to per capita value transaction from 161.58 US dollars in 1999 to 135.74 US dollars in 2000 to 135.19 USD in 2000 and touched a low of 70.20 USD in 2003. However, it once again regained in 2004 with 104.62, a 15% increase in 2004 when compared to 10.1% in 2003.

It can be concluded that emerging markets witnessed a notable increase in per capita spending as rising levels of disposable income and developing banking systems encouraged operators and issuers to look beyond the constraints of mature, developed markets. This is visible from the per capita consumption value of Singapore which has grown from 1371.02 in 1999 to 2011.77 in 2004, with the growth rate of 20.3%, Hong Kong, from 2230.98 in 1999 to 3524.75 in 2004 with a growth rate of 20.1% and Japan from 1334.26 in 1999 to 1886.94 in 2004 with a growth rate of 20.2%.

Thus, the growth rate of credit cards has shown tremendous potential throughout the world undergoing a major transformation from paper based transaction to credit card transaction. It should also be noted that major banking reforms in many developing countries has resulted in such major transformations, which again could be linked to globalization process occurring throughout the world.

Table 7
Country-wise Credit Cards and Per Capita Value Transaction Distribution

(US dollar per head)

Country	1999	2000	2001	2002	2003	2004	Number of Times Increase*
Canada	3827.19 (14.6)	3985.39 (15.2)	3931.40 (15.0)	4002.78 (15.3)	4780.18 (18.3)	5658.14 (21.6)	1.5
USA	3795.50 (13.6)	4318.10 (15.4)	4523.31 (16.2)	4792.78 (17.1)	5088.94 (18.2)	5432.18 (19.4)	1.4
Hong Kong China	2230.98 (12.7)	2692.51 (15.4)	3019.47 (17.2)	3049.47 (17.4)	3020.81 (17.2)	3524.75 (20.1)	1.6
Australia	2053.98 (9.4)	2325.53 (10.6)	2467.65 (11.3)	3620.05 (16.6)	4841.89 (22.2)	6532.52 (29.9)	3.2
U.K.	1927.07 (12.8)	2011.42 (13.4)	2074.16 (13.8)	2427.00 (16.2)	2953.25 (19.7)	3628.92 (24.2)	1.9
Israel	1656.35 (14.3)	1831.10 (15.8)	1934.72 (16.7)	1858.11 (16.1)	2039.28 (17.6)	2241.71 (19.3)	1.3
Singapore	1371.02 (13.8)	1571.50 (15.8)	1561.69 (15.7)	1671.68 (16.8)	1735.17 (17.5)	2011.77 (20.3)	1.5
Japan	1334.26 (14.2)	1523.47 (16.3)	1439.60 (15.4)	1476.74 (15.8)	1702.60 (18.2)	1886.94 (20.2)	1.4
Taiwan	876.51 (11.2)	1060.11 (13.5)	1177.13 (15.0)	1292.51 (16.5)	1511.76 (19.3)	1921.37 (24.5)	2.2

Contd.

Country	*1999*	*2000*	*2001*	*2002*	*2003*	*2004*	*Number of Times Increase**
Portugal	641.97	710.88	705.69	834.67	1063.19	1320.60	2.0
	(12.2)	(13.5)	(13.4)	(15.8)	(20.1)	(25.0)	
Venezuela	161.58	135.74	135.19	90.53	70.20	104.62	0.6
	(23.2)	(19.5)	(19.4)	(13.0)	(10.1)	(15.0)	
Malaysia	145.76	198.17	241.83	288.54	333.95	379.07	2.6
	(12.1)	(16.4)	(20.0)	(23.9)	(27.6)	(31.4)	

Source: Financial Cards: World, Euromonitor International, 2004.
*shows the number of times increase in 2004 when compared to 1999 in terms of percentage shown within brackets.

With this background, it would also be useful to know the interest rates charged by different countries on account of credit card usage.

Table 8
Country-Wise Interest Rates on Credit Cards

Country	*Annual Interest Rate (in %)*
India	35.4
U.S.	16.0
U.K.	15.0
Japan	13.0
Taiwan	19.0
Thailand	19.0
Malaysia	24.0
Singapore	24.0

Source: *http://groups.google.co.in/group/soc.culture.indian*

Table 8 shows the different rates charged by different countries on swiping credit cards by the cardholders. It can be seen that India charges a very high rate when compared to other countries which are comparatively low per year. The explanations given by issuing banks for a high charge are low transaction volume, low card penetration, Indian's preference for cash over cards–still conservatism to a certain degree dominating. Next comes Malaysia and Singapore with 24%, all the above three countries falling under Asia-Pacific region. A general conclusion that could be made thus is that developing Asian-Pacific countries have a higher interest rates on credit cards than developed countries. With this background, it would be useful to venture into the scope in Asia-Pacific region.

SCOPE IN ASIA–PACIFIC REGION

Asia-Pacific's strong growth took it to the top of the list of the world's most valuable regional markets.

Figure 4 shows that the largest share of potentiality has been held by the Asia-Pacific region with 32.2% followed by Western Europe (27.9%) and North America (25.9%).

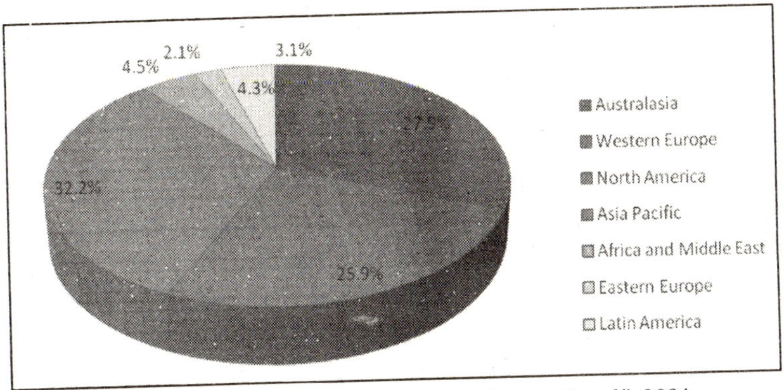

Source: Financial Cards: World, "Euromonitor International", 2004.

Figure 4 : Regional Market Share of Credit Cards for the Year 2004

Table 9
Country-wise Distribution of Cards Per Bankable Population - 2004

(Per Person)

Country	*Cards/Bankable Population in 2005*
Korea	3.00
Taiwan	2.66
Hong Kong	2.00
Singapore	1.1
Malaysia	0.4
India	0.03

Source: www.ibef.org, 2005

Table 9 shows cards per bankable population in Asia-Pacific countries. From the table it is quite clear that cards per bankable population is very low in India, at a meager 0.03 level whereas in other Asian Pacific countries of Korea, Hong Kong, Singapore and Malaysia, the scores are considerably higher. In Malaysia, it is 0.4, but still the score is above 0.1, much higher than the Indian level of 0.03. Thus, the table emphasizes the fact that banking habits of the people of India need to be improved which will thereby provide a lot of scope of credit card usage. More the banking habits by the people, higher will be the development of the economy, with greater transparency.

Table 10
Cards Spend in Asia Pacific Countries-2005

(Per card in US dollars)

Country	*Cards Spend - 2005*
India	Less than 500
Srilanka	800
Hong Kong & Singapore	3000

Source: NCAER, "Development of Electronic Payments in India", 2005.

Table 10 shows that with regard to cards spend too, that is expending from a credit card, India stands at a relatively low level. As of 2007 beginning, it was still just over 2 per cent, while that for comparable economies, it stood at 10-12 per cent.

Table 11
Distribution of Outstanding Balances Per Card - 2005

(In Billions US Dollars)

Country	*Outstanding Balance in 2005*
India	1.5
Korea	90.0
Hong Kong	10.0
Malaysia	2.5

Source: *www.ibef.org, 2005.*

Table 11 shows the outstanding balances in India in comparison to other Asia-Pacific countries. Here too, the outstanding balances in India are much lower at 1.5 billions whereas even in Malaysia it is 2.5 billion dollars and Korea shows the highest of 90 billion dollars. This table also reveals the ample scope left for India to expand in the credit card sector.

Also, compared to other Asian countries, the Indian market lags in terms of card spending and outstanding. The card market is at a nascent stage. Total card spending in India is only at around 1.22% (2005) of the Asian spending, which is estimated to be $400 billion.

Table 12 shows the percentage owning credit cards by different countries. When compared to UAE and Kuwait, India shows a very low value of 14% only. Since only around 30% to 35% live in the urban area and within this, only the middle and high income group hold credit cards, the percentage is very small. Hence India has to expand in all spheres i.e. economically and socially to remove inequalities in urban and rural areas and among different sections in the urban sector too in order to increase the number to use credit cards. Only education and technology can make this dream come true.

Table 12
Percentage Owning Credit Cards - 2005

Country	*Percentage (%)*
India	14
UAE	63
Kuwait	50

Source: MasterCard International Survey, 2005.

Table 13 shows the personal consumption expenditure through credit cards for the year 2005. Whereas Korea has a very high personal consumption expenditure of 19% followed by Hong Kong, it is extremely low comparatively in India, and is just 0.4%. This shows that people are yet to come out of their shell in expending through credit cards and there is still huge potential to be tapped for the better usage of the credit cards.

Thus it is clear that Asia-Pacific region offers significant potential for banking services, with a vast population of over 3 billion. *INDIA alone account for over 1 million, which is largely under-banked*. The high growth rates of economic activity and the burgeoning consumer financial services sector are attracting increased activity from both domestic and international players.

Since the study pertains to Chennai city which belongs to India, an overall review of India as part of Asia Pacific region has also been touched upon by the researcher to have a detailed and broader view before delving into study of India.

Table 13
Personal Consumption Expenditure by Using Credit Cards - 2005

Country	*Outstanding Balance in 2005*
India	0.4
U.S.	9.0
Hong Kong	15.0
Korea	19.0

Source: Business India, January 17-30, 2005.

INDIA AS PART OF ASIA-PACIFIC REGION

India comes under the Asia-Pacific region, more precisely, it belongs to part of South Asia. India is a developing country and is strongly becoming an emerging market in the global scenario though a majority of the population relies on agriculture. Banking forms the backbone to the economy's financial system and the loyalty placed by Indian people on banks is more and strong. However, it is also a point to be noted that when compared to other countries percentage of population holding a bank account, is comparatively low. Table 14 below explains this fact.

Table 14 shows the distribution of bank account holder's different countries in 2004, as studied by visa international. The table shows that more and more a country is developed, more the people hold a bank account and vice versa. On such terms, though we can argue that countries like Malaysia and Singapore are developing countries in terms of credit cards acceptance, usage and performance, they have educational

Table 14
Distribution of Bank Account Holders - 2004

Country	*% Population with Bank Account*
Germany	98
Singapore	95
United Kingdom	91
United States	88
Japan	85
Canada	85
Australia	85
Ireland	63
Malaysia	55
Argentina	49
South Africa	46
Mexico	35
Poland	30
Egypt	23
India	20

Source: Visa International and Global Insight, "Payment Solutions for Modernizing Economies", 2004.

level much higher when compared to countries like India. However, India is a country which constantly emphasis the role of education and technology in the development of the country and also practices the same by trying to improve educational levels and imparting of education from the age 3 through various measures and government schemes. Technological adaption and adoption also has been a welcoming feature to make India a supreme country by 2020 as per the dreams of our ex-president Dr. Abdul Kalam. When education and technology join hands, usage of credit cards will receive a red-carpet welcome as issuers view *India and China* as a vast potential market in the *Asian Region*.

Figures 5 and 6 show the distribution of credit cards per '000 capita and percentage of adult population holding credit card account respectively. It can be seen that both are quite low in India. Thus tapping the unbanked population and increasing the number of people holding and using credit cards is quite large thereby enabling to enhance the efficient and transparent working of the economy.

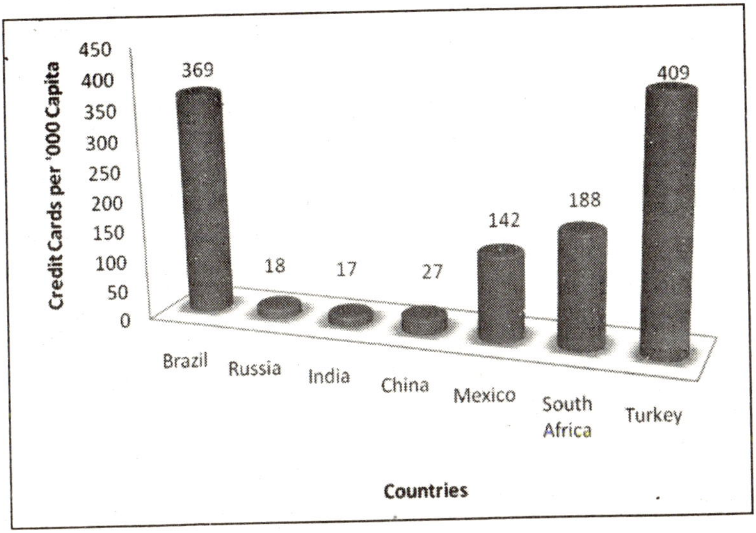

Source: Merrill Lynch Estimates, February 2007.

Figure 5 : Distribution of Credit Cards Per '000 Capita

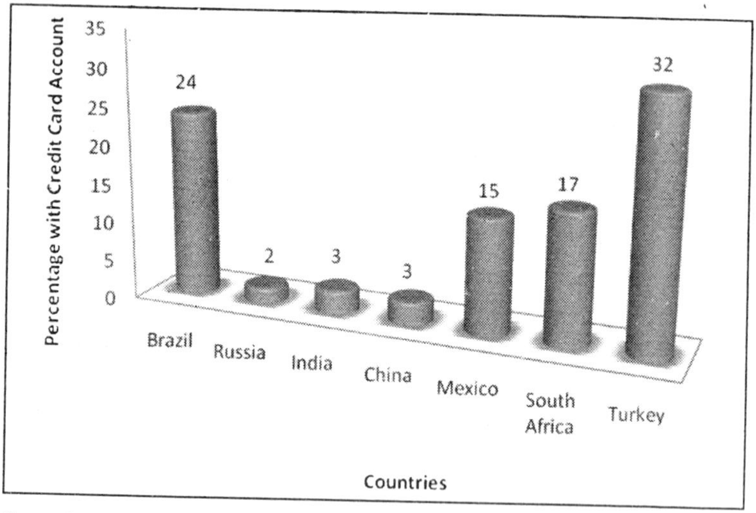

Source: Merrill Lynch Estimates, February 2007.

Figure 6 : Distribution Showing Percentage of Adult Population with Credit Card Account

There is growth in all parts of the world and there is no slowing down and the same holds good to India too. The segment performance of credit cards has registered an impressive growth rate and India is the only country in the Asia-Pacific region that has registered a double-digit growth in the credit cards segment. Thus, having a glimpse of the global scenario, it would be vital to throw light on the impact of reforms, particularly the banking reforms in India and therefore its impact on the economy.

NOTES

1. Handbook On Credit Cards, Indian Banks Association Publications, Chennai, 2006. www.indianbank.com
2. First data International, "What could First Data mean for you?", Card World and Fraud Watch Annual User Guide–*International Journal for the Card, Financial and Retail Services*, C&M Publications Ltd, U.K., 2005.
3. Ted Lacobuzio (2006), "The Cashless, Cardless Society", European Card Review, ECR Publishing Partnership LLP, Volume 13, Number 12.

4

IMPACT OF REFORMS ON CREDIT CARD SYSTEM IN INDIA

GROWTH OF CREDIT CARD INDUSTRY IN INDIA SINCE 1991

Card Industry in general and the Credit Card Industry in particular owe its growth to the banking sector reforms in India which occurred with the advent of the New Economic Policy of 1991. Because, it was these reforms that gave some freedom to the banks governing credit card business.

Every interest rate pertaining to bank lending were decided by RBI but when it came to interest rate charged on credit card dues, RBI gave total freedom to banks, to decide their own rate of interest. This led to most of the banks charging interest rate as high as 36% p.a. This attractive rate prompted more and more banks to join the Credit Card band wagon since the spread in this business was far more than they could have ever bargained for, in traditional banking.

The entry of new private sector banks like ICICI, HDFC, UTI Bank (now AXIS Bank), IDBI etc. was primarily as a result of the banking sector reforms since these banks were highly tech-savvy right from day one and were also restricting their clientele only to the top layer. They could afford to restrict their clientele to profitable business alone right from the beginning. As a result, these banks could register large profits and high growth rates during the first five to six years of their existence. Having established a reputation for high growth and profitability, these banks had to sustain them to maintain their credibility. In their search for new avenues for profitable business, they identified Credit Card as one area with high potential for profits and growth. This also led to the growth of Cards Industry in India, though, in all fairness, credit should go to older public sector banks (PSBs) and multinational banks like Citibank, Standard Chartered Bank, etc., for laying the foundations of Credit Card Industry in India.

Indian Credit Card business is growing at a relative speed with a fierce battle between the banks to enter into the wallets of the Indian middle class. The following table shows the amazing growth of credit cards in our country from a mere 5.5 million in 2001 to around 26.5 million by 2006.

Table 1
Cards in Circulation in India

(in Millions)

Year	*Number of Cards in Circulation*
2001	5.5
2002	7.4
2003	9.7
2004	14.2
2005	19.6
2006	26.5

Source: "Credit Card Transactions–India", Euromonitor International, Trade Press, March 2007.

Table 1 shows that there has been a gradual growth in the number of cards being in circulation, the number of cards being in force being about 26.5 million in 2006 when compared to 5.5 million in 2001 and the number is expected to be 30 per cent more in 2007-2008. Bankers expect their credit card business to grow by over 30 per cent in 2007-2008. This wider acceptance can be attributed mainly to two facts. First, bankers attribute the increasing acceptance of cards to the fact that it does not require a high capital deployment. Second, prompt payment by most consumers is an added advantage.[1]

Moreover, in the words of Sachin Khandelwal, *"Innovative schemes and offers to cardholders, along with various partner merchants and circulation of more co-branded cards, with added benefits on specific usages have benefited the customers encouraging more and more people to use it."*[2]

Credit Card business is turning to be quite competitive and banks in India, in their bid to build volumes rapidly are taking credit card culture to the masses, not just restricting to bigger cities alone but even to smaller cities and towns. *"Competition"*, they say, *"is a compelling force which makes even monoliths to make new moves"*. In the age of consumerism, customer is the king and the banking sector has, of late, woken up to the fact that offering products and services tailored to meet the customers' specific needs can actually bring in more business.

Banks today do much more than lending and borrowing money. The private sector banks can be said to be the forerunners in offering customer-oriented service. However, public sector banks too, are slowly but steadily catching up with their private counterparts. SBI with its 7 associates constitute the largest cash-spewing network in the country.

A Credit Card can also be used to contribute money to a worthy cause. For this, one needs a card that has a tie-up with a non-profit making Non Government Organization (NGO). SBI has tied up with four such NGOs, the Cancer Patients Aid Association, the National Association for the Blind, SOS Children's Villages (helping the children) of India and the World Wildlife Fund (WWF) for Nature in India. Similarly, Citibank has a tie-up with Child Relief and You (CRY) and WWF. SBI has also introduced the Kisan Credit Cards (KCC), which, however, does not function like a credit card in the strictest sense of the term, but the farmer is liable to use it for availing seeds, fertilizer, machinery etc., according to his needs.

Thus Credit Cards has changed the way people look at money. And to carve to the changing spending spree, lifestyle and living pattern, banks are learning more about their customers in order to be able to offer them services they really want today and needless to say, credit cards does perfectly fit to bridge this gap.

CURRENT TREND AND SCENARIO

Credit Card or the Plastic Money, as it is popularly referred to, was slow to enter the Indian market because of the high sentimental value that Indian consumers attach to cash. Credit cards arrived in India about two decades ago. In the early stages its growth was very slow in terms of volume and value. Even the number of players were limited. Even SBI, India's largest bank, despite its widespread reach, has aggressively started promoting credit cards only three years ago.

However, in the recent past, the scenario has changed dramatically. The card market in the country is set to witness unprecedented growth. Spends on credit cards are likely to see a three-fold jump, according to current growth estimates. VISA is looking at volumes, depending on the growth of the market.

An under-penetrated market, a growing middle-class, new channels of cards, new segments and new categories are expected to be major drivers of this growth. Figure 1 below

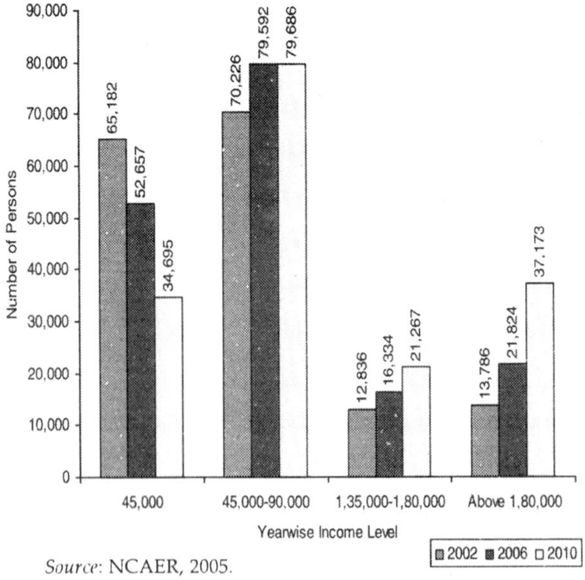

Source: NCAER, 2005.

Figure 1: Income Levels of Households in India

shows how *"Consumer India"* became a global attraction – India's middle class of 300 million, became not just one the of the largest markets, but a global phenomenon. India has a considerable number of rich and their number is growing[3].

Figure 1 shows the different income group levels in India for the period 2002 to 2006 and the estimated number of persons in each group for the same period has been predicted for 2010. The figures not only show the growing income levels of the people but also the number of people falling under the lower income level keeps decreasing and the number of persons falling under the next higher income category keeps increasing.

Whereas in 2002, persons falling under the income level Rs. 45,000 were 65,182, it is expected to fall to 34,695 in 2010 which would mean that they are likely to fall under the next higher income category of Rs. 45,000 – Rs. 90,000. Similarly, more will come under the first level of income group, that is, to Rs.45,000 from a lower income level. Thus the disposable income shows a rising trend from figure 1 which goes to prove the fact that the number of people with more spending capacity is growing in India. Higher the disposable income, higher the level of expenses that will be expended as consumers strive to maintain their status quo with those who are at par.

According to NCAER report, the very rich with an annual income of over Rs.2,15,000 will increase from one million to 6.2 million households by 2006-07; the consuming class with an annual income of Rs. 45,000 – Rs. 2,15,000 will grow from 28.6 million to 90.9 million households and the number of households in the Aspirants, that is, annual income level between Rs.16,000 – Rs. 22,000 and destitute (< Rs. 16,000) groups will decrease significantly during the same period.[4]

Table 2 shows that the disposable income in the hands of the people of India has been and is still on the rise, thanks to the Information Technology Sector, as many are opting for this sector. Obviously, there has been a general feeling amongst people and reality shows that this industry too is on the boom and compared to other sectors' income levels, income earned by those in this sector is considerably high. However, this is just one part of the scenario. Increasing incomes and inflationary effects, both being the cause and the effect to each other, the general income levels of an average Indian has been on the rise, be it in any department, be it skilled or semi skilled. With the incomes on the rise, the spending pattern and the spending method has also undergone a lot of change and here plays the role of credit cards for the increased expenditure pattern of the consumers.

Table 2
Disposable Income in India-2006

(Rs. Million)

Year	*Disposable Income*	*Percentage Growth*
2001	15735.6	5.0
2002	17395.5	1.2
2003	18778.4	23.6
2004	20293.4	57.4
2005	21293.1	7.3
2006	21839.6	14.2

Source: Financial Cards–India Euromonitor International, Trade Press, March 2007.

With the above mentioned vital statistics, in India, most of the players in the market have now started offering cards to an increasing number of Tier II cities. Also with increasing marketing spends and more merchant terminals being set up, the card industry is likely to see a sharp growth; it has been estimated to increase to 35 million by 2010 and retail sales volume from debit and credit cards are likely to grow at 30% if taken at compounded annual growth rate.

There is immense growth potential in the domestic card industry. A glance at the Indian population reveals that India's middle/upper middle class, which is the target segment, represents a population of over 10 million. There are only 2 to 3 million cardholders in this segment (32% on an average), each possessing an average of two cards. This is a very low figure given India's huge middle to upper middle class population. With the total population of over one billion, just 1.4% of the total population are credit card holders. There is no doubt that the domestic card industry is yet to mature and offers significant long-term growth potential.

Given the lack of maturity of the domestic card industry, its growth will depend upon building core retail business, with more sophisticated products. In the expansion of the domestic credit card market, the existing foreign players and nationalized banks, and the new domestic private sector banks are expected to play an important role with complementary strategies. The efforts of these banks will be to increase the card base.

A TRIANGULAR PERSPECTIVE OF CREDIT CARD SYSTEM IN INDIA

Consumers' Perspective

It is not only the campaigns of the credit card companies which have lured the people to the *"Cult of Credit'* but the main factor, perhaps, has been in the profound transformation of attitudes towards savings and debt.

Credit cards have influenced household strategies due to the re-organization of macro policies. Thus, credit cards have definitely made a dent in the culturally oriented cognitive

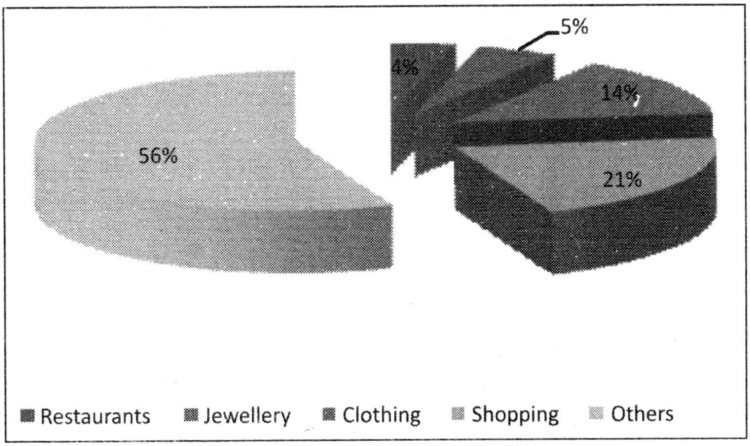

Source: ICICI Properties Research and Market Estimates, 2005

Figure 2: Spending Pattern

connect between earnings and consumption. Credit cards have come to define one's consumption over employment decisions due to a temporary absence of financial constraints, the rational response for which is to enhance the individual's identity and social status through the cloak of credit-financed consumption.

Figure 2 shows the spending pattern as of 2005 on various heads like shopping, restaurants, clothing, jewellery etc. by consumers in India through credit cards. The figure shows that credit cards which were once used only for prestigious items like jewellery accounts now for just 5% and expenses through credit cards for various other purposes have increased to 56%.

CONSUMPTION PATTERN IN INDIA

If consumption is growing, it is evident that incomes are growing too, and consequently so is the spending power of the consumer. The average Indian income has been growing at frenetic pace over the years. Spending is always based on needs. The needs hamper of the average Indian has changed tremendously after the government enforced economic reforms 15 years ago. In 1991, 80% of the spending was on fixed items.

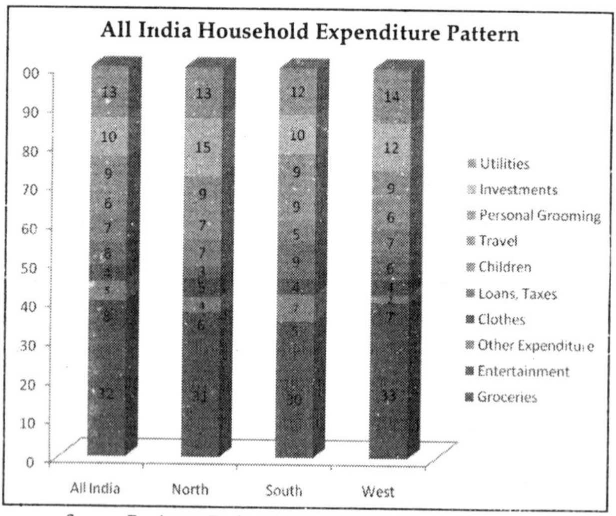

Source: Business Today, November 20, 2005.

Figure 3: All India Household Expenditure Pattern

Today, the basket comprises many high tech items too like mobile handsets, gifts and consumer durables.

Figure 3 vividly depicts that Indian consumers, taken region-wise separately, or on a national level, spend the most (over 30%) on groceries, followed by utilities (13%), then by Investments (10%), which means that Indians are more prone to savings and thereby in various types of investments for future security, followed by other heads as given in the key indicator. However, it is also worth noting that spends on entertainment and personal grooming has also started taking place in his expenditure pattern which is a clear sign of the changing mentality of an average Indian who otherwise is not much known for such expenses. A gradual change has definitely started occurring in the mind set of Indians, gradually and carefully growing and nourishing – this considerable nourishment being implanted and watered by the introduction of credit cards and the culture of credit card.

Table 3
Itemwise Distribution of Credit Card Expenditure

Sector	*Expenditure Incurred in 2006*
Food and Drink	44,649.5
Motoring	58,044.4
Other retailers	33,487.1
Household	49,114.5
Travel	42,417.0
Clothing and Footwear	1,11,623.8
Entertainment	35,719.6
Hotels	37,952.1

Source : Euromonitor International, Trade Press – Financial Cards, India. March 2007.

In correlation to the pie diagram 2 and bar diagram 3, the study made by Euromonitor International[2] as given in table 4.6 suggests that Indian consumers are no more shying away from expending, instead, have started using their credit cards for various purposes. This is also an example of growing income in the hands of the younger generation thereby contributing to the growth of credit card potentiality since the attitude of the youngsters have become different and they want to live the life more comfortably.

Indian consumers prefer to use plastic money to cash payments for shopping and eating out. Payments cards had grown from 3 million to more than 44 million in the last ten years. Credit card usage has gone up too. The consistent growth of consumer market being ripe in India goes to prove that it should be a key incentive for any manufacturer wanting to sell his wares in India.[6]

Overflowing malls, crowded jewellery shops, and the soaring sales of durables show that we have arrived as a nation of whole-hearted spenders. If higher incomes and the general state of well-being could have triggered the willingness to splurge, credit cards have made it only so much easier. Economist concur that our growth could well be significantly consumption-driven. The spending Indian is now the centerpiece. The young, growing earning population is likely to move faster down this road, armed with credit card.[7]

Collation of Consumption Pattern to Consumer Needs

Producers produce goods and services for consumption. Advertising enables the information of these goods and services to reach consumers. This would then translate into buying decisions if the consumer can afford it or need it. However, often the need is created by enticing the consumer to purchase and consume. Advertising and marketing not only makes people consume more but is also responsible for the consumption of luxuries, which are, many a times, sophisticated, costlier alternatives.

Today is the age of commoditised business. Credit cards give the consumer a reason to use a product, in this age of plastic. The latest slogan of the consumer is, "it is never too early to save for tomorrow and never too late as long as one has earnings at their disposal". Hence, as long as they are able to manage judiciously their credit lines, credit cards come handy for their trendy lifestyle.

Moreover, consumption in India is at its zenith. Spending patterns in the Indian economy is probably at one of its high levels. Excess money is spent more on luxury goods like higher tourism spends, strong demand for gold, demand for housing etc. apart from usual luxury goods such as trendy, fancy, clothes, car, mobile connections etc. High prices seem to be no obstacle for the consumer. The soaring income levels and the upcoming youngsters has thus transformed into a "vulnerable generation". In India, there has been a steady increase of 35–40%[8] p.a. of credit card usage. The credit card boom has been an important attributing factor to peer pressure. Over 600 cities and small towns across the country have enterprises and organizations which accept credit cards.

Table 4
Performance of Personal Credit Cards in India

	2001	*2002*	*2003*	*2004*	*2005*	*2006*
Number of transactions (million)	25.3	36.9	53.0	75.7	104.3	141.3
Transaction value (Rupees million)	71,436.5	1,04,264.5	1,49,300.0	2,11,655.0	2,91,234.3	3,92,947.1

Source: Credit Card Transactions-India, Euromonitor International, March 2007.

Table 4 shows the performance of personal credit cards sector in India for the period 2001-2006. Personal credit cards refer to the individual persons holding credit cards. This is an important factor because there are different types of credit cards like the corporate cards, gift cards etc. which do not depict the expenditure of the individuals directly and does not come under the purview of knowing the transparency of the expenditures expended by the individuals. Table 4 shows that both the number of transactions and its value have increased gradually from 2001 and it has stood six times more in 2006 in terms of number of transactions and four times in terms of transaction value.

Table 5 shows that CAGR of personal credit card sector performance has shown an impressive growth of 41.1% during the periods 2001-2006 in terms of transactions number and in terms of value, at 40.6% during the same said years.

Table 5
Percentage Growth of Personal Credit Cards Sector

% Growth	*2005-2006*	*2001-06 CAGR**
Number of transactions	35.4	41.1
Transaction value	34.9	40.6

Source: Euromonitor International, Credit Card Transactions, India, March 2007.
*Compounded Annual Growth Rate.

The above two tables, namely table 4 and table 5 show that on an overall basis the personal credit card sector performance has shown direct and immense growth supported by the percentage growth wherein the transaction value also has been on the rise. This is a welcoming feature both for the sector and for the economy as such since more and more individuals of the nation come under direct scrutiny when more and more is expended through credit cards.

Financial Independence is a catchphrase of modern life and this depends on two things: life stage and lifestyle. With this qualification, it can be conceived as having ownership of an adequate corpus of resources to meet the lifestyle needs at any given life stage of the individual.[9] And in the hands of the changing lifestyle, *Plastic Money* has become a valid weapon to dance to the tune of modern generation.

MERCHANT'S PERSPECTIVE

To increase the penetration of credit cards in India, it becomes imperative for the retailers too, to have a changed mindset. Retailers need to understand that credit cards is like a service offered by him to his customer which will have long term benefits in terms of increased purchase, better customer loyalty in the long run and preventing the loss of current customer.

The credit card has offered benefits just not for the consumers alone, but for the retailers too. A versatile, reliable credit card processing service can help a retailer's business increase sales by enabling him to accept all forms of payment from anywhere at any time. A valuable service will offer security protection by utilizing modern encryption technology. Apart from business, customer-retention is his ultimate goal.

This being the situation, it is worth looking into merchant's side of getting his cash when a deal gets finalized. This can be categorized into two:

(a) Before the introduction of EDC

(b) The current EDC system

Before the Introduction of Electronic Data Coding System (EDC)

Initially, when a card was swiped in the zip-zap machine, a customer enjoyed a clean credit of 45 to 60 days which varied from bank to bank. The merchant received his payment from his banker when he presented the statement of the purchases made. The bankers in turn, would send the vouchers to their respective Head Office or clearing offices where the money is collected from banks that had issued the cards. The whole process took around 21 days whereas the credit enjoyed by the customer was much more than that. Such a system had two disadvantages viz:

- Not enough balance in account of the customer
- Payment to merchants not immediate

Current EDC System

The above stated problems are no more in vogue, thanks to the introduction of EDC system, and neither the merchants need to neither wait for his payment, for the EDC machines gives results in seconds nor lose his customer and sales.

As soon as a card is swiped in the EDC, the transaction is referred to the main server of the bank and it is then routed to the respective VISA / MASTER Saver. The result is displayed in seconds, 4 or 5 seconds, to be precise. During this brief period, the credit limit availed; limit available and the authenticity of the card are checked. The signature on the card is to be checked by the shop owner or the acceptor with the signature on the counterfoil. Forgery is also minimized with the introduction of photo cards. The merchants receive their payments immediately or the next day, on production of their bills to the bank. Since the balance amount is also checked by the EDC server, the shopkeeper can also be rest assured that his transaction has passed with no complication. In case there is no enough balance, the EDC machine rejects the card stating that it is already full. Swiping does not take place at all under such a situation and the shopkeeper is safe of any fraudulent activity. It is also a message to the customer, both for his usage of card and to make his part payment to reuse his card elsewhere.

On having understood the mechanics behind the swiping of a credit card and its acceptance as cash by a merchant, it would be worthwhile to know the POS mechanics too. By POS is meant Point of Sale. It means the place and time at which a transaction occurs. This term also refers to the devices or software used to capture transactions. The POS terminals include a reader to detect the magnetic stripe on a bank card, a key board and a telephone connection to a payment processing network.[10]

Table 6 gives the industry spends of credit cards at Point of Sale (POS). The Credit Card industry in India consists of only banks and hence the various banks and their industry spend from 2003 to 2006 has been given. All banks have shown a positive trend in their industry spend on credit cards which show that many merchants are accepting credit cards. HDFC has shown tremendous growth of 65.9% in 2006 from a meager 2.2% in 2003, 30 times higher in growth rate within a short span of three years followed by ICICI Bank at 58.8% in 2006 from 3.5% in 2003, 16.8 times the growth within the same period. The third position has been occupied by SBI which has shown 43.6% increase in the industry spend in 2006 from 15.6% in 2003, 2.8 times the growth rate within three years span. The figures show that privatization has helped banks in India to grow at a larger scale, specially in the field of credit card sector since private Indian Banks (HDFC & ICICI) have taken the rein from MNCs followed by the major public sector bank of India, the SBI. It is also evident that banks in India are competitive and efficient when competing with MNCs. This is a good sign for the economy. Hence, we can also say that merchants are willing to accept any bank's credit card as long as they have reliance on the bank. However, the rate of use of certain bank's credit card depends on the tie up between the bank and the merchant, or specific reasons like festive seasons wherein the banks offer some kind of discount of one type or the other to intuiting the cardholder to swipe their card or due to some promotional activities undertaken either by the bank or the merchant for a particular bank credit card for reason whatsoever.

Table 6
Bank-wise Spend at the Pos*

(In Crores)

Banks	*Year* 2003	2004	2005	2006	*Number of Times Increase***
ICICI	1,200	2376	10,570.00	20,152.4	16.8
	(3.5)	(6.9)	(30.8)	(58.8)	
Citibank	4,505	3,000	6,750.00	8,284.09	1.84
	(20.0)	(13.3)	(29.9)	(36.8)	
HDFC	270	750	3,104.52	7,975.87	30.0
	(2.2)	(6.2)	(25.7)	(65.9)	
SBI	2,405	2500	3,811.75	6,726.59	2.8
	(15.6)	(16.2)	(24.7)	(43.6)	
StanChart	3,000	3000	4,075.40	5,176.78	
	(19.7)	(19.7)	(26.7)	(33.9)	1.7
HSBC	1,560	1800	1,800.00	2745.43	
	(19.7)	(22.8)	(22.8)	(34.7)	1.8
ABN AMRO	200	1200	1,750.00	2,552.08	
	(3.5)	(21.0)	(30.7)	(44.8)	12.8
Vijaya Bank	–	–	417.78	562.01	
Andhra Bank	132	178	225.00	284.41	2.2
	(16.1)	(21.7)	(27.5)	(34.7)	
Bank of India	297	400	178.00	268.5	0.9
	(26.0)	(25.0)	(15.6)	(23.5)	
Amex	1920	2160	–	–	
Bank of Baroda	144	160	122.50	186.84	1.3
	(23.5)	(26.1)	(20.0)	(30.5)	
Central Bank	96	113	147.00	150.21	1.6
of India	(19.0)	(22.3)	(29.0)	(29.7)	
Others	238	238	162.31	177.52	0.7
	(29.2)	(29.2)	(19.9)	(21.8)	
Total	16,118	20555	33,339.06	55,525.58	3.5
	(21.3)	(27.2)	(44.1)	(73.5)	

Source: Payment Card Industry, Venture Infotek Research Publication, 2006. *www.ventureinfotek.com*
* POS-Point of sale
** and figures in brackets calculated by the researcher. It shows the percentage approximated to the nearest tens after the first decimal.

Cards are witnessing a gradual expansion in Tier II and Tier III cities and it is more important to get more merchants in smaller markets to accept cards without charging anything extra for card usage.[11]

However, despite the above features being explicit for a merchant establishment to accept a credit card, he may not do so on certain instances such as for many small retailers, not accepting credit cards is a way to ensure that transactions are unrecorded–and therefore, savings of taxes; for small ticket items, the retailer himself might discourage customers from swiping a credit card; charges levied for a card is quite high which has to be borne by the retailer, for not on all occasions can it be passed to the customers; in many smaller cities and towns, leave alone its penetration in rural areas, credit card payment are yet to get penetrated.

Of late, card companies are looking at small towns to expand the power of plastic and their success hinges on merchant acceptance. Merchant establishments have seen a growth of 40% in the last year. The concentration of POS terminals has increased, which is a good sign towards the progress of the industry as a whole.

At present the top six metropolitan cities of Mumbai, Delhi, Kolkata, Chennai, Hyderabad and Bangalore account for 65% of all the payment card spends, the remainder coming from smaller cities like Ahmadabad, Chandigarh, Coimbatore and tourist destinations.

Financial Reforms on Banks

"Banking Reform is critical to the health of national economy and global financial markets" observed Lawrence Sacz.

Banking has evolved a long way from the days of the medieval moneylenders to the present scenario, where it is hard to trail the trace of money from the beginning to the end. The trail starts right from the small server leaving a few rupees in his local bank to the billions of rupee loans raised by banks and financial institutions, capable of financing projects in any country in the world. Still, these banking majors are heavily dependent upon their retail business as global competition intensified.

The issue of retail banking is extremely important and topical and is perceived to be the in-thing in today's world of banking. The concept of 'Retail Banking' is quite broad in nature – it refers to the dealing of commercial banks with individual customers, both on liabilities and assets sided of the balance sheet. Today's retail banking sector is characterized by three basic characteristics:

- Multiple products (deposit, *Credit Cards*, insurance, investments and securities).
- Multiple channels of distribution (Call centre, branch internet etc.)
- Multiple customer groups (consumer, small business and corporate).[12]

This is not a new phenomenon and has always been prevalent in India in various forms. For the last few years it has become synonymous with mainstream banking for many banks. The typical products offered in the Indian retail banking segment are Housing Loans, Consumption Loans, Auto Loans, *Credit Cards*. Some of the basic reasons that could be highlighted are economic prosperity and the consequent increase in purchasing power has given a fillip to a consumer boom; changing consumer demographics indicate vast potential for growth in consumption, both qualitatively and quantitatively, technological factors like innovations relating to increased use of credit/debit cards, ATMs etc; treasury income of the banks has been on the decline, a scenario which provides a good vehicle of profit maximization and decline in interest rates. In this backdrop, two specific domains of retail lending in India are: *Credit Cards and Housing*.

An issuer is a provider of a bank card to a cardholder authorizing that person to use it to complete financial transactions. Banks are the lone issuers of credit cards as far as India is concerned. Table 7 shows the total number of credit cards issued by banks and that many banks are in the arena of issuing credit cards and the rate at which they have been issuing have been slowly but steadily increasing, on an average by all banks. There has been a total increase of 34.7% (3.5 times

Table 7
Bank-wise Number of Cards in Circulation

(Thousand Cards)

Bank	*2001*	*2002*	*2003*	*2004*	*2005*	*Number of Times the Growth**
ICICI Bank Ltd	455.7	1066.8	2052.9	3668.8	5075.4	11.1
	(3.7)	(8.7)	(16.7)	(29.8)	(41.2)	
Citibank India	1458.1	1648.6	2052.9	2623.2	3213.7	2.2
	(13.3)	(15.0)	(18.7)	(23.9)	(29.2)	
StanChart Bank India	1275.9	1328.6	1353.0	1788.5	2400.5	1.9
	(15.7)	(16.3)	(16.6)	(22.0)	(29.5)	
SBI Cards & Payment Services Ltd	741.6	1097.2	1097.5	1408.0	2106.06	2.8
	(11.5)	(17.0)	(17.0)	(21.8)	(32.7)	
HDFC Bank Ltd	–	140.4	447.5	1035.3	1469.7	10.6
		(4.5)	(14.5)	(33.5)	(47.5)	
HSBC India	535.9	630.4	699.8	917.2	1234.5	2.3
	(13.3)	(15.7)	(17.4)	(22.8)	(30.7)	
Amex Co	321.7	465.5	559.9	715.4	979.8	3.0
ABN AMRO Bank NV	–	109.7	337.7	579.8	960.2	8.8
		(5.5)	(17.0)	(29.2)	(48.3)	
Canara Bank	72.5	93.9	88.7	248.5	431.1	5.9
	(7.8)	(10.0)	(9.5)	(26.6)	(46.1)	
Bank of India	139.3	121.1	168.9	186.4	323.3	2.3
	(14.8)	(12.9)	(18.0)	(19.9)	(34.4)	
Bank of Baroda	123.6	158.0	168.9	215.3	284.1	2.3
	(13.0)	(16.6)	(17.8)	(22.7)	(29.9)	

Contd.

Bank	*2001*	*2002*	*2003*	*2004*	*2005*	*Number of Times the Growth**
Others	385.8	539.8	672.6	813.8	1117.0	2.9
	(10.9)	(15.3)	(19.1)	(23.1)	(31.7)	
Total	5510.0	7400.0	9700.0	14200.0	19596.0	3.5
	(9.8)	(13.1)	(17.2)	(25.2)	(34.7)	

Source: Credit Card Transactions-India, Euromonitor International, Trade Press, March 2007.
* and percentage shown within brackets, calculated by the researcher, approximated to the nearest tens place after the first decimal.

in 2005 when compared to 2001) in the number of cards issued by all issuers taken together. All banks have shown a positive relationship in their increase in 2005 when compared to 2001 and it is noteworthy to show that public sector banks like Canara Bank with 46.1%, Bank of India with 34.4% are in the lead competing equally with the private sector banks and other MNC banks. This shows the improvement in the growth of credit card sector, which once again can be attributed to the reason of liberalization policy adopted by banks after NEP, 1991. They have boldly ventured into a competitive market, which until 1991 had been restricted to a limited circle. This is supported by the table wherein it can be seen that, on an average, all banks have grown minimum twice in issuance in 2006 when compared to 2001.

Table 8
Operator-wise Number of Cards in India

(Thousand Cards)

Banks	*2001*	*2002*	*2003*	*2004*	*2005*
Visa International Service Association	28817.7	3907.2	5189.5	7668.0	10797.4
MasterCard International Inc	2325.2	3063.6	3909.1	5637.4	7544.5
American Express Co.	165.3	229.4	320.1	482.8	666.3
Citibank India	137.8	199.8	281 3	411.8	587.9
Total	5510.0	7400.0	9700.0	14200.0	19596.0

Source:Credit Card Transactions-India, Euromonitor International, Trade Press, March 2007.

Table 9
Operator-wise Transaction Value

(Rupees Million)

Operator	*2001*	*2002*	*2003*	*2004*	*2005*
Visa International Service Association	41226.7	59158.0	83425.5	116998.1	160338.7
MasterÇard International Inc	30693.8	43787.3	61866.9	87095.9	119605.8
American Express Co	4519.1	6933.7	11333.3	17933.6	26494.9
Citibank India	3788.1	6290.4	9666.8	14473.5	21144.5
Total	80299.6	116169.5	166292.5	236501.0	327583.8

Source: Credit Card Transactions-India, Euromonitor International, Trade Press, March 2007.

The Tables 8 and 9 approve the fact that the operators too have been steadily increasing the number of approvals of credit cards. Also the four companies are foreign organizations and again, their bold venture into India could be attributed to the impact of globalization, liberalization and privatization process in India because it has been only due to these key factors that foreign direct investments (FDI), have started pouring in India. The green signal given to banks after NEP 1991 and financial reforms gave a congenial atmosphere for these operators to enter Indian market.

Table 10
Bank-wise Credit Card Transactions in India

(Million Transactions)

Banks	*2001*	*2002*	*2003*	*2004*	*2005*
HDFC Bank Ltd.	–	3.0	8.2	14.8	24.9
Citibank India	10.6	12.1	14.2	17.1	19.9
ICICI Bank Ltd	–	1.9	4.4	11.3	19.5
BOB	6.6	8.1	11.0	14.1	16.7
IDBI Bank Ltd	–	1.1	2.7	5.1	7.9
UTI Bank (now AXIS)	2.1	3.1	4.1	5.8	7.8
Bank of India	1.6	2.3	3.0	4.3	5.8
Others	5.6	7.0	7.9	6.7	7.2

Source: Credit Card Transactions India, Euromonitor International, Trade Press, March 2007.

An acquirer (or a banker) is a financial institution that supports merchants by providing services for processing card transactions. In terms of these lines, we find from the table 10 that the bankers have been increasing their support to the merchants through the years. Contrarily, if merchants do not support these financial institutions by accepting these services, credit card acceptance would not have been on the rise. Table 10 shows the credit cards transactions by the acquirers (banks in India) for the period 2001 to 2005 and is indicative of the fact that sellers' market is highly dependent on buyers' demand.

ICICI bank holds a percentage growth of 70.9 in 2005 when compared to 2004. This may be attributed to the various sales techniques like advertising adopted by this bank to reach the mass, be it the credit cardholder or the merchant. All banks in general show prospective growth percentage with HDFC Bank leading the list in the second position, next only to ICICI with 66.7 % followed by IDBI Bank Ltd with 53.1%. The overall growth per cent has been 37.8% for the year ending 2005 when compared to 2004.

Table 11
Bank-wise Personal Credit Cards Transactions in India

(Million Transactions)

Banks	*2001*	*2002*	*2003*	*2004*	*2005*	*Number of Times the Growth**
HDFC Bank Ltd.	–	3.0	8.0	14.4	24.0	8
		(6.1)	(16.2)	(29.1)	(48.6)	
Citibank India	10.1	11.4	13.3	15.9	18.2	1.8
	(14.7)	(16.5)	(19.3)	(23.1)	(26.4)	
ICICI Bank Ltd.	–	1.8	4.2	11.0	18.8	10.5
		(5.0)	(7.3)	(30.7)	(52.5)	
BOB	6.3	7.7	10.6	13.6	16.2	2.6
	(11.6)	(14.2)	(19.5)	(25.0)	(29.8)	
IDBI Bank Ltd.	–	1.1	2.7	4.9	7.5	6.8
		(6.8)	(16.7)	(30.2)	(46.3)	
UTI Bank(now AXIS)	2.0	3.0	4.0	5.7	7.5	3.8
	(9.0)	(13.5)	(18.0)	(25.7)	(33.8)	
Bank of India	1.5	2.2	2.9	4.2	5.7	3.8
	(9.0)	(13.3)	(17.6)	(25.5)	(34.5)	
Others	5.3	6.6	7.4	6.1	6.4	1.2
	(16.7)	(20.8)	(23.3)	(19.2)	(20.1)	
Total	25.3	36.9	53.0	75.7	104.3	4.1
	(8.6)	(12.5)	(18.0)	(25.6)	(35.3)	

Source: Credit Card Transactions-India, Euromonitor International, Trade Press, March 2007.
* and figures within brackets calculated by the researcher, shows the percentage and number of times the growth in 2005 when compared to 2001.

Table 12 shows the personal credit cards transactionsvalue by different operators for the periods ranging from 2001 to 2005. The table shows that in total, this value has increased to Rs. 2,91,234.3 million in 2005 from Rs.71,436.5 million in 2001.

Table 12
Operator-wise Personal Credit Cards in India

(Rupees Million)

Acquirer	*2001*	*2002*	*2003*	*2004*	*2005*
Visa International Service Association	37,502.2	54,217.5	76,441.6	1,06,885.8	1,45,617.1
MasterCard International Inc	27,503.1	39,620.5	55,987.5	78,524.0	1,07,174.2
American Express Co	3,571.8	5,241.8	9,107.3	14,604.2	21,551.3
Citibank India	2,857.5	5,004.7	7,763.6	11,641.0	16,891.6
Total	71,436.5	1,04,264.5	1,49,300.0	2,11,655.0	2,91,234.3

Source: Credit Card Transactions-India, Euromonitor International, Trade Press, March 2007.

Though credit card transactions table gives only an overall view, it is the personal credit cards transaction which shows the real picture since it deals with individuals' holding credit cards. Personal credit cards transactions show the consumption pattern, consumer behavior, rationality behind using credit cards by the consumers indirectly, and the increasing trend directly relating to the merchant acceptance. It is only the above which gives the transparent functioning of the economy. Viewing from this aspect, it is clear from tables 8, 9 and 12 that the transaction value by operators has been rising which means more and more issuance of credit cards for circulation in the economy. Higher the circulation of credit cards more the transparency and more efficiency can be put forth by the government for regulating the country.

Credit Card Sector Performance in Banks

While usage of cards by customers of banks in India has been in vogue since the mid-1980, it is only since early 1990's, to be more precise since the inception of the NEP of 1991, that the market has witnessed a quantum jump. The total number of cards issued by banks and outstanding, increased from 2.69 crore as on end December 2003 to 4.33 crore as on end December 2004. The actual usage too had registered increase both in terms of volume and value.

Table 13 shows the volume and value of retail electronic and card based transactions in India for the years 2000 to 2006. Although cash continues to be used heavily in retail transactions in India, the use of cheques and several other payment instruments such as credit cards, debit cards etc. on the whole has been increasing in recent years. The use of payment cards, both in volume and value terms, more than doubled in 2004-05 compared to previous year and the same holds for 2005-06 when compared to 2004-2005.

Table 13
Volume and Value of Retail Electronic and Card Based Transactions

	Volume in Thousands				*Value in Crores*	
	Retail Electronic @		*Card Based#*		*Total*	
Year 1	*Volume* 2	*Value* 3	*Volume* 4	*Value* 5	*Volume* 6	*Value* 7
2000-01	N.A.	N.A.	N.A.	N.A.	N.A.	N.A.
2001-02	17,770	6,123	N.A.	N.A.	17,770	6,123
2002-03	23,660	10,222	N.A.	N.A.	23,660	10,222
2003-04	29,046	29,933	1,85,501	35,870	2,14,547	65,803
2004-05	57,071	79,479	3,62,040	77,120	4,19,111	2,30,500
2005-06	83,200 (832)	1,06,599	(10,453)	2,36,994	(11,286)	3,43,593

Source: Report on Trend and Progress of Banking in India, 2005-06, Supplement to RBI Bulletin.
Key
N.A. = Not Available
@ = ECS (Debit & Credit), EFT & SEFT
# = Credit Cards, Debit Cards and Smart Cards.

Note: Volume represents number of transactions.

As a result of sharp increase in electronic transactions, the proportion of electronic transaction both in volume and value terms has increased sharply. This has been explained in table 14 and figure 3 below.

Table 14 shows that the electronic based transactions, have, within a short span of time, increased from 173 million in 2002-03 to 11,300 million in 2005-06. The corresponding value earned from electronic transactions has also shown considerable increase. Corresponding paper based value has shown significant decrease from 1,34,24,313 crores to 1,13,37,062 crores which further proves the point that increase in electronic payment system is on the rise.

Table 14
Paper Based Versus Electronic Based Transactions

	Volume (in Million)			*Value (In Crores of Rupees)*		
Year	*Paper Based*	*Electronic Based*	*Total*	*Paper Based*	*Electronic Based 6*	*Total*
1	2	3	4	5	6	7
2002-03	1,014	173	1,187	1,34,24,313	37,536	1,34,61,849
2003-04	1,023	274	1,247	1,15,94,976	67,352	1,16,62,328
2004-05	1,125	432	1,557	1,10,47,052	42,24,746	1,52,71,798
2005-06	12,895	11,300	24,195	1,13,37,062	1,18,84,429	2,32,21,491

Source: Report on Trend and Progress of Banking in India, 2005-06, Supplement to RBI Bulletin.

Reflecting the increasing use of electronic and card-based payment in retail transactions, their share in total transactions constituted 46.7% in terms of volume and 51.2% in terms of value in 2006.

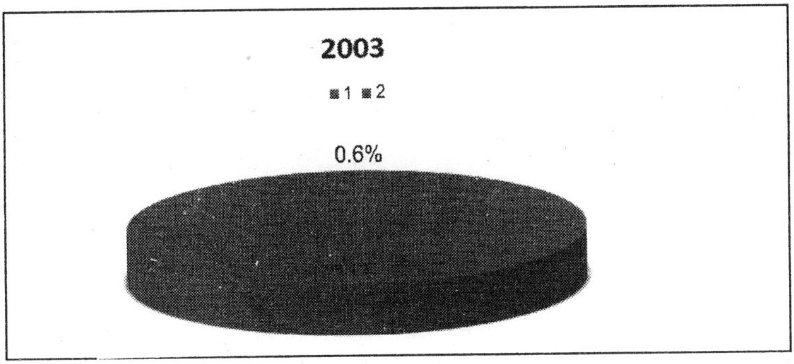

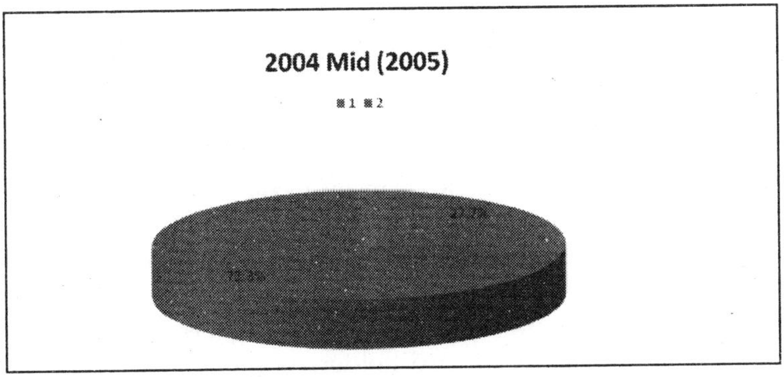

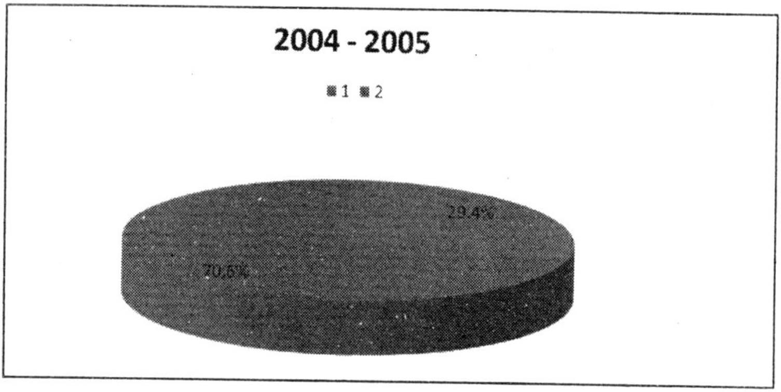

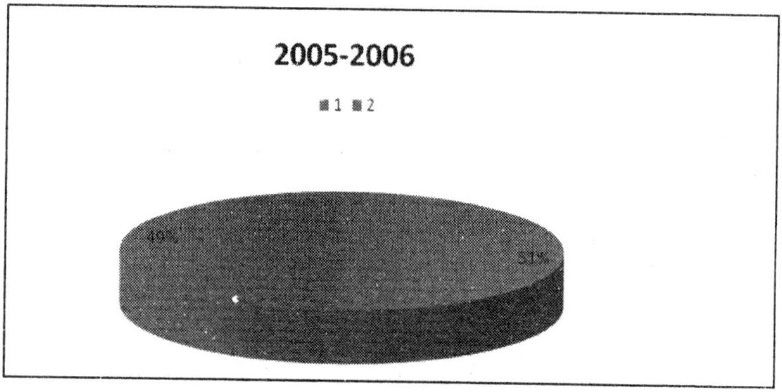

Key: 1 = Paper Based Transaction
2 = Electronic Transaction

Figure 4 : Relative Flows (value) of Paper based vs Electronic Transactions

Convenience and easy acceptability of credit cards and technological advances have resulted in continuous rise in retail electronic and card-based mode of payment.

Almost all categories of banks issue credit cards. It has found greater acceptance in terms of usage in the major cities of the country, with the four major metropolitan cities accounting for the bulk of the transactions, Chennai being one among the four.

However, when it comes to issuing credit cards to customers, Indian credit card holders pay one of the highest interest rates globally, and if they use their card as a means to roll over credit, it means a high profit segment for the banks. And this excludes the hidden costs.

Banks and Credit Cards Receivables

A bank receiving its payment from its customer with respect to the bank's credit card being used is called *Receivables* by the banks. Thus, all the payments made by its customers on using the respective bank's credit card that day (single day) will be the *Total Credit Card Receivables of the Bank.*

Table 15
Credit Card Receivables of Banks

		As % of Outstanding Loans	
Items	*Amount Outstanding (in Rupees Billion)*	*Impaired Credit*	*Net Profitable Assets*
Credit Card Receivables	61.67	6.3	2.4

Source: RBI report on 'Trends and Progress of banking in India", Business & economy, 9 Sep.– 22 Sep, 2005, p. 28.

Table 15 shows the credit card receivables by the banks of India for the year ending 2005 which gives a net profitable asset of 2.4%.

The primary job of banks is accepting deposits for the purpose of lending and investments. SPREAD (the gap between the interest paid to the depositor and the interest charged from the borrower) is quite low and the scope for increasing it is limited. Banks started looking other avenues for increasing this profitability. They also felt that they would also bring in/attract more clientele into their fold. They offered various ancillary services and one among such services in the retail segment is the Credit Card Segment. The point why all banks make such aggressive moves into the credit card market is attributed to the fact that globally around half of the profits of the consumer banks come from credit cards and factors that would contribute to bring down profits for any card company is NPAs or the delinquencies in the cards industry which is estimated to be approximately around 8.5% to 10 %, much below the industry average, and spends on cards.

SEGMENT PERFORMANCE IN INDIA

"The credit card segment in India has registered an impressive growth rate of around 30% this year"–Indian Card Industry Survey, 2006.[13]

Table 16
Performance of Credit Card Sector

Year	Transactions (Million)	Outstanding (Rs. Millions)	Value (Rs. Millions)	Spend (%value) Domestic	Spend (%value) Foreign	Value of Internet Transactions (Million)
2001	26.4	21,059.9	80,299.6	–	–	220.6
2002	38.6	25,339.0	1,16,169.5	–	–	390.1
2003	55.4	31,200.0	1,66,292.5	–	–	659.9
2004	79.2	43,750.0	2,36,501.0	–	–	1,086.7
2005	109.6	67,500.0	3,27,583.8	–	–	1,725.2
2006	149.2	1,07,325.0	4,46,495.2	88.1	11.9	2,659.5

Source: Euromonitor International, Trade Press – Financial Transactions, India. March 2007.

Table 16 shows clearly the rising use of credit cards in India over the years. There has been an increase both in terms of transactions and value arising thereof on usage of credit cards. Also, there has been a substantial increase in the usage of credit cards in internet transactions too.

Table 17
Percentage Growth Rate of Personal Credit Cards

% Growth	2001-06	2001-06 CAGR	2001-06 Total
Number of transactions (million)	35.4	41.1	459.6
Transactions Value (Rupees million)	34.9	40.6	450.1

Source: Euromonitor International, Trade Press – Financial Transactions, India. March 2007.

Table 17 depicts the personal credit cards sector performance for the years 2001 to 2006. The number of transactions and its value shows a promising figure of growth.

There are over 180 lakh credit cards in use in India and the pattern of usage is also undergoing a sea change. This rapid growth can be attributed to the aggressive issuance of credit cards by top five players in the industry, and seven banks with a portfolio of over 10 lakh credit cards each, namely, *ICICI, CITIBANK, SBI,STANCHART, HDFC, HSBC* and *ABN Amro.*

Table 18 depicts that on an average all the banks, be it public sector, private sector or multinational bank, have increased the issuance of credit cards. This presents the direct fact that there is potentiality in India and there has been an increase in the card usage by the people. Apart from the above banks, some of the key banks like AXIS (then called UTI) Bank, J&K Bank, Union Bank of India, PNB etc. launched their cards in the year 2005-2006.[14] From the table it can also be shown that, except for Bank of India, all other banks show an estimated positive growth in 2007 vis-à-vis 2006. The healthy factor that can be seen is that State Bank of India (SBI) is expected to increase the number of credit cards (in lakhs) by 15.94 by 2007 end, which is the largest and the first ever launched bank in India and which belongs to the public sector bank. If not for the usage of consumers, SBI cannot be expected to increase its market share. Hence, the competitive edge has been finely handled by an Indian public sector bank, thanks to the banking sector reforms ushered by NEP of 1991.

Table 19 shows the different banks playing a crucial role in the issuance of credit cards. MNC banks, public sector banks and private sector banks are all included to have a better analysis for the period ranging from 2002 to 2006 and the approximate estimated value for year ending 2007 has also been predicted.

The Private Sector Banks exhibited a phenomenal growth in the credit card market with card issuance valuating by 37% and the card base rising from 49.33 lakh in 2005 to 67.79 lakhs in 2006. Public Sector Banks have shown a 37% increase in the base and MNC banks have shown the least growth of 15%.[15] This shows that there is increased participation by the banks of India (both private and public sector banks), which again seems to be a welcoming feature. However the MNC banks are still the overall leaders which account for about 40% of

Table 18
Distribution of Banks-wise Credit Card Usage

No. of Cards (in lakhs)

Bank	Year 2002 2	2003 3	2004 4	2005 5	2006 6	2007* 7	Expected Increase/ Decrease in 2007 (7-6) 8**
ICICI	5.00	11.00	14.30	36.71	51.39	60.24	+8.85
Citibank	16.00	17.00	22.00	27.00	28.18	36.63	+8.45
State Bank of India	9.03	12.50	16.25	19.75	26.56	42.50	+15.94
StanChart	12.70	13.70	15.00	19.00	21.70	24.81	+3.11
HDFC	-	1.80	2.34	12.62	16.40	22.14	+5.74
HSBC	5.88	6.50	9.00	9.00	11.35	13.38	+2.03
ABN AMRO	-	-	-	7.00	10.10	20.13	+10.03
Bank of Baroda	1.50	1.80	2.16	3.50	4.63	6.14	+1.51
Canara Bank	0.88	1.01	1.21	2.10	2.26	2.36	+0.1
Bank of India	1.69	1.38	1.46	1.40	1.67	1.52	-0.15
Andhra Bank	1.03	0.64	0.77	1.55	1.66	1.70	+0.04
Vijaya bank	0.74	0.93	1.11	0.70	0.82	0.86	+0.04
CBI	-	0.74	3.00	0.50	0.41	0.40	+0.01
Syndicate	-	-	-	0.24	0.26	0.29	+0.03
Others	0.73	1.17	1.87	0.17	2.69	3.23	+0.54
TFL	0.67	0.77	0.92	-	-	-	-

Source: Payment Card Industry, 2006. www.ventureinfotek.com
* does not include 2007
** Calculated by the researcher

credit card industry in India. This could be contributed to the advantage gained by foreigners to open and market their products, here the credit cards, due to globalization impact. If not for globalization and liberalization, there would not have been a stiff competition rendered by the public and private sector banks in India to issue credit cards, woo to increase credit card usage of their banks vis a vis to multinational banks. Similarly, between the private sector and the public sector banks of India, private sector banks like the HDFC and the ICICI have shown a spectacular growth in increasing their card base. This has been possible only due to privatization and the banking reforms undertaken after the introduction of NEP of 1991 and thereby its recommendations.

Table 19
Analysis in terms of MNC, Private andPublic Sector Players

(Number in lakhs)

Bank	*2002*	*2003*	*2004*	*2005*	*2006*	*2007**
			MNC			
Citibank	16.00	17.00	22.00	27.00	28.18	36.63
StanChart	12.70	13.70	15.00	19.00	21.7	24.81
HSBC	5.388	6.50	9.00	9.00	11.35	13.36
AMEX	3.53	4.80	5.25	–	–	–
ABN	–	1.25	2.25	7.00	10.1	20.13
Total	38.11	43.25	53.50	62.00	71.33	94.95
			Private			
ICICI	5.00	11.00	14.30	36.71	51.39	60.24
HDFC	–	1.80	2.34	12.621	16.4	22.14
TFL	0.67	0.77	0.92	–	–	–
Total	5.67	13.57	17.50	49.33	67.79	82.38
			Public			
SBI	9.03	12.50	16.25	19.75	26.56	42.50
BOB	1.50	1.80	2.16	3.50	4.63	6.14
BOI	1.69	1.38	1.46	1.40	1.67	1.52
Vijaya	0.74	0.93	1.11	0.70	0.82	0.86
Andhra	1.03	0.64	0.77	1.55	1.66	1.70
Canara	0.88	1.01	1.21	2.10	2.26	2.36
CBI	–	0.74	3.00	2.10	2.26	2.36
Syndicate	–	–	–	0.24	0.26	0.29
Others	0.73	1.17	1.87	0.17	2.69	3.23
Total	15.60	20.16	27.83	29.91	40.96	59.00

Source: Payment Card Industry, 2003 and 2006, Venture Infotek Research Publication. *www.ventureinfotek.com*

* Estimated value.

BOOMING INDUSTRY

The Payment Industry is undergoing a mixed transformation. It is boom time for the plastic card market. Credit Card issuances and the number of places where one can use these have increased. And the willingness to spend is also on the rise. Indians were sold 45,000 credit cards a day in 2004 and together they spent Rs.120 crore a day through credit cards during the year.

Visa together with 33 member financial institutions issues approximately 23 million payment cards in the country with both debit and credit cards growing at an average rate of 50%.[16] The value of credit card transactions grew by 36% in 2006, up by 35% from 2005.

The banks have also realized that having a large number of cards in circulation is not enough, especially in a country where very less use the roll over payment system which is not profitable to the banks or the issuers and acquirers. The issuing banks are offering incentives to encourage card usage. A few of the issuers are now targeting the affluent class by developing special cards just for them, which are marketed as prestige card, to make the holders feel special. Many issuers are also into co-branding their credit cards with various companies for better scope, which helps in increased usage of credit cards.

"The future of credit cards in India is safe, given that the e-commerce market is showing great growth potential" opines *Euromonitor International*: Country Sector Briefing, in its Credit Card Transactions–India review.[17] It also says that "although other modes of payment on the internet are rising, the traditional method has always been to use credit cards and this is going to be forward".

Table 20 shows that the general potentiality of credit cards in terms of volume and value is going to be on the rise, be it personal or internet transactions. The rise in the level of internet transactions indicate the level of technology that has provided so much sophistication to man who can finalize a dealing with the click of a button on the computer. This also indicates the versatile nature of India to adopt and adapt itself to the growing global importance of technology, thanks to globalization and liberalization as far as this sector is concerned.

Table 20
Future of Credit Cards 2007-2011

Year	Transactions (Million)	Value of Transactions (Rupees Million)	Internet Transactions No. of Accounts ('000 Accounts)	Internet Transactions Mn Trans.	Internet Transactions Value (Rs Mn)
2006	149.2	4,46,495.2	10,354.0	3.8	2,659.5
2007	194.1	5,84,918.1	12,265.3	5.5	3,935.2
2008	234.4	6,94,089.3	14,514.1	7.9	5,779.5
2009	257.7	7,82,064.4	17,050.5	11.3	8,245.2
2010	284.4	8,37,409.7	20,008.0	15.1	11,198.9
2011	309.8	8,77,497.6	23,244.2	19.4	14,875.5

Source: Euromonitor International, Financial Cards–India, March 2007.

Table 20 depicts a very rosy picture of the potentiality of credit cards in India as a whole. There appears to be a rising trend of the usage of credit cards, transactions that will be made by this plastic money, both directly with the merchants or through internet for purchase of goods and services. This would mean proceeding towards the right path for the economy as already described earlier leading to a more transparent economy, thereby helping in its efficient functioning. However, it should also be noted that credit cards are a means of convenience, and therefore, more defaulting would mean a digress and not a progress for the economy as much of the money of the banks which could be used for better purposes of lending would be blocked and turn out to be bad debts to be written off if the consumers are found bankrupt and could not pay a part, if not the whole amount, even in their near future. Hence, as long as the money thus circulating does not turn out be credit card debt traps, there seems to be a very bright future for this sector.

In India, currently there are 155.32 lakh credit card holders. The number has increased by 37% from last year's 103.87 lakhs.

Such being the background, there has arisen an opportunity for this sector to grow which has led to the opening of a manufacturing and production unit in Chennai.

With the growing importance of Credit Card payment in India, Versatile Card Technology India (P) Limited, began its operation in 2000. The company owns the credit of the first of its kind in India and of date, many such card manufacturing companies are growing.

Table 21
Production of Cards in India

(In Millions)

Year	*Number*
2002	300
2006	450

Source: Versatile Card Technology, Information Brochure, Chennai, 2006.

Table 21 shows the number of cards produced in India alone which has stood at 450 million by 2006 and around 90% is said to be produced for global demand of which more than 70 million caters to domestic demand for Credit Cards. Another fact to be noted here is that the opening of production unit could be correlated to the industrial reforms that were introduced after the inception of NEP 1991, wherein many restrictions were removed since this unit began as an Export Oriented Unit (EOU) in 2000.

Having seen the production side, a quick glance about the per capita credit card performance in India would be worth knowing.

Table 22 shows that the per capita credit card performance, though when compared to developed countries and other emerging markets is quite low, shows a steady increase throughout the years under review. With continuing strong economic conditions, rising affluence and purchasing power, more credit eligible Indian consumers are expected to make payments with credit cards, with the fastest growth coming from smaller towns and cities. This supports the fact that there is untapped potential in India for credit cards to perform and hence it becomes important to study the credit card system in India.

Table 22
Per Capita Credit Card Performance in India

Year	*Per Capita Performance*
1999	0.84
2000	1.75
2001	2.01
2002	2.23
2003	2.69
2004	3.66

Source: Financial Cards: World, "Euromonitor International", 2004

Development of Electronic Payment Systems in India

With the opening of the Indian economy by the NEP 1991 and reforms in the financial sector, the value of electronic payments too gained importance. Electronic payments systems include transactions through credit cards, debit cards, ATM cards, prepaid cards and smart cards. This has been on the rise which will be evident from Figure 6.

Figure 5 shows that the electronic clearing system which was 67.4 crores in 1999 shot up to Rs. 9,976 crores in 2004. This

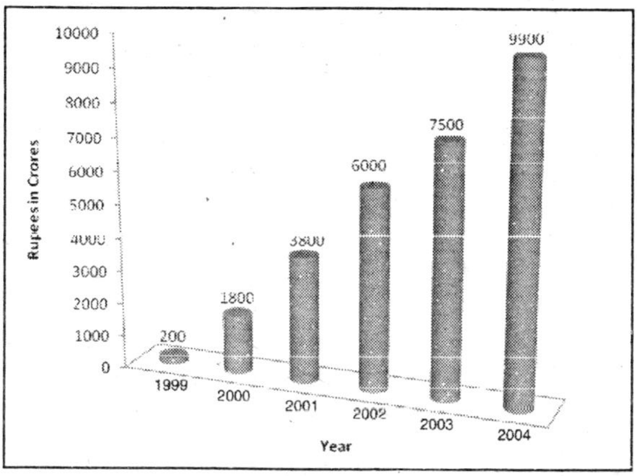

Source: RBI Annual Report (2003-04)

Figure 5: Value of Electronic Payment Transactions 1999–2004

shows the Aftermath of NEP 1991 reforms in the banking sector through the acceptance and growth of electronic payment systems[18].

With increasing disposable income, a rise in consumer expenditure and technological advances in the banking sector, India has witnessed tremendous growth in payment card usage. This is depicted in Figure 6.

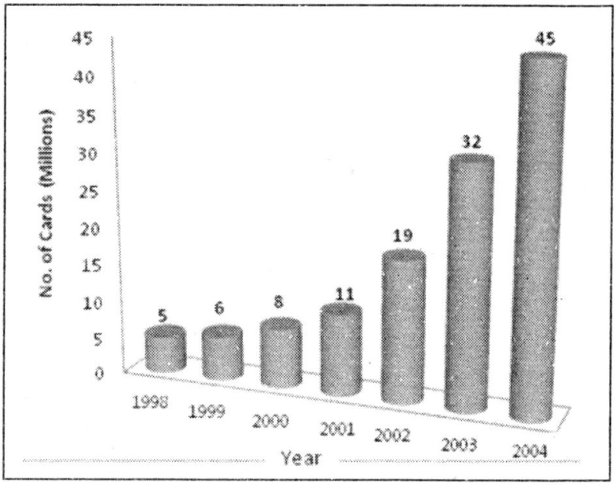

Figure 6: Growth in Payment Cards in India 1998–2004

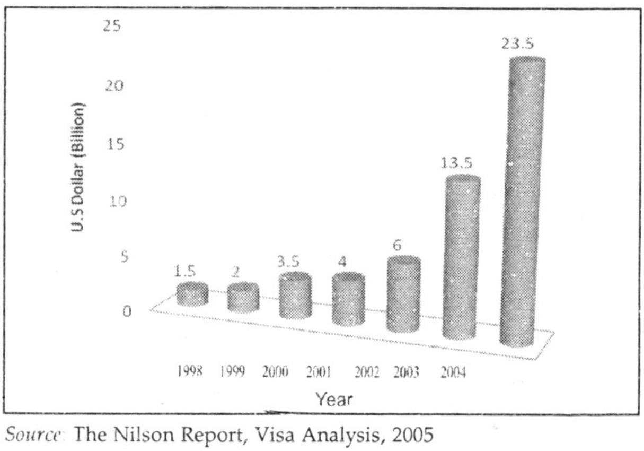

Source: The Nilson Report, Visa Analysis, 2005

Figure 7: Total Card Usage 1998 - 2004

Figure 6 show that India's payment card system which is barely two decades old has shown tremendous growth with more than 14 million credit cards today. It has grown at a compounded annualized growth rate of 55%.

Figure 7 shows an increase in the total card usage through the years 1998-2004 which reached 23.5 billion US dollars in 2004 from a mere 1.5 billion US dollars in 1998.

Merchant acceptance network, a key driver for the growth of card payments has also been showing an increasing trend.

Figure 8 shows a slow and steady growth of merchant acceptance. As the number of card-accepting merchants increase, there is more scope for the expansion of the card payment system. This also highlights the fact that consumers

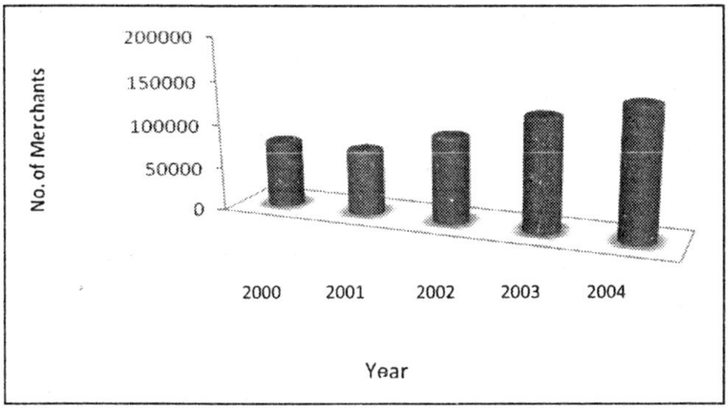

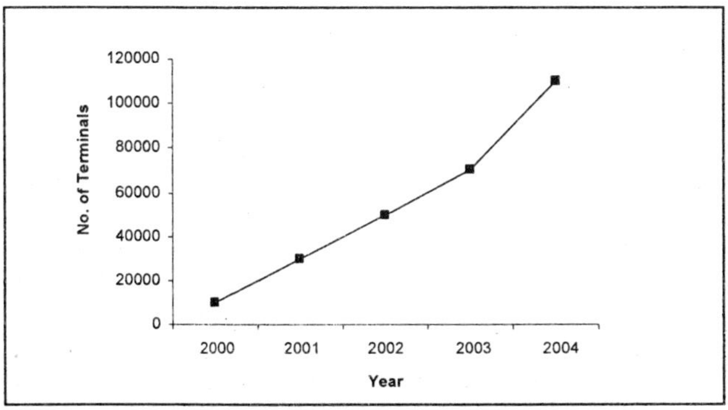

Source: Venture Infotek Research, 2004. (NCAER report, 2005)

Figure 8 : Merchant Acceptance 2000–2004

have slowly started shifting their expenditure through electronic payments from very rare or important or bulky items to common items like household expenditures. Thus, with increasing card usage and merchant acceptance there is lot of scope for the banks to improve its productivity through technology and efficiency with its unbanked population of 80% still remaining. Being the second largest populated country in the world and with growing young, dynamic, entrepreneurs, and Indian banks can go a lot forward with full charge. One such solution lies in the credit card sector of the retail banking segment of the banks.

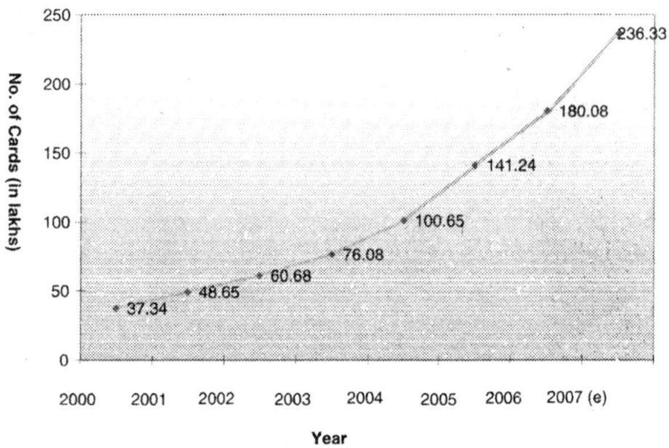

Source: Indian Payment Card Industry, Venture Infotek Research Publication, 2006.

Figure 9: Growth of Credit Cards Issued

India is the second largest new growth market, after China. India's wealthy families have an estimated $560 billion in assets and China's have more than $700 million. With such being the scenario, India has a tremendous potential in the Credit Card Market Segment.

Before concluding, *it is worth noting that India is one of the fastest growing markets for credit cards since*[19]

(a) Over 16 million credit cards are in circulation in the hands of 5 million people across India.

(b) There are over 1,80,000 POS terminals, slated to hit 2,50,000 by 2007 end.

(c) Nearly Rs.2,20,000 crore was withdrawn by credit card users in 2005 through ATMs.

(d) 73% of Indians were spending less than Rs.1,600 approximately using their cards in 2005.

(e) Less than 0.6% of the personal consumption expenditure in India is through cards as against 16% in the US. Thus, there is a huge potential to tap.

With the above statistics and having browsed upon the performance in India, it becomes important to study such a growing sector with reference to Chennai. Thus a brief profile of Tamil Nadu which has its capital city as Chennai, and that of Chennai city too becomes equally vital.

NOTES

1. Shobha Kannan, *"The Hindu Business Line"*, ePaper, July, 2007. *http://www.blonnet.com/2007/07/19/stories/*2007071951010600.htm
2. Sachin Khandelwal, *"The Hindu Business Line"*, ePaper, July 19, 2007. *http://www.blonnet.com/2007/07/19/stories/200 7071951 010600.htm*
3. Abhijit Sen (2005), *"Business Today Special,* 15th Anniversary Issue, Informedia India Publishers, New Delhi, January 17.
4. NCAER, "Development of Electronic Payment Systems in India", a published white paper, January 2005.
5. Financial Cards : India, Euromonitor International, a published market survey, March 2007.
6. IBEF, "Consumer Markets – Selling to India" www.ibef.org
7. Uma Shashikant (2005), "Spending Spree", Outlook Money, Outlook Publishing (India) Pvt. Ltd., Chennai, November 30.
8. Raghu Mohan (2005), "Plastic Smiles", Business India, Raheja Group of Publications, January.
9. Niranjan Krishnan (2005), "Financial Independence –What's That", Investors India, Bajaj Capital Group of Publications, Mumbai, August.
10. *www.indianbank.com,* "Handbook on Credit Cards", 2006.
11. Khandelwal, "Credit card business set for over 30% growth", Business Line, ePaper, July 19, 2007. *http://www.blonnet.com/2007/07/19/stories/2007071951010600.htm*

12. Shyamala Gopinath (2005), "Retail Banking–Opportunities and Challenges", *RBI Bulletin*, June.

    Smt. Shyamala Gopinath was Deputy Governor, Reserve Bank of India as a Key Note Speaker at the IBA–Banking Frontiers International Conference on "Retail Banking Directions: Opportunities & Challenges" at Mumbai on May 28, 2005.

13. *www.ventureinfotek.com*
14. *www.ventureinfotek.com*, "Payment Card Industry", Venture Infotek Research Publication, 2006.
15. "Payment Card Industry", Venture Infotek Research Publication, 2006. *www.ventureinfotek.com*,
16. Raghu Mohan (2005), "Plastic Smiles–Industry Report", Business India, Infomedia Publishers (P) Limited, New Delhi, January 17-30, p. 62.
17. Euromonitor International, Financial Cards: India, a published market survey report, March 2007.
18. NCAER, "Development of Electronic Payment Systems in India", a published white paper, 2004.
19. Dayamanti Datta (2006), "Plastic Promise", India Today, Living Media Publications Limited, Chennai, March 27, pp. 76–80.

5

ANALYSES AND INTERPRETATION

INTRODUCTION

Credit cards play a vital and pivotal role in today's modern economy, thereby influencing the market structure as a whole, both from the customers' side and the merchants' side, with the key part being played by the banks who issue these cards. Though it can be concluded that Chennai city is no more a conservative city in terms of spending, acquiring comfort, and the stringent savings mentality has been relaxed, thanks to the growing young income earning group in the middle-class sector, irrespective of gender, it may not be totally concluded as well that the spirit of spending has made this class spendthrift as we go deeper into our analysis.

Before the study launches into the analyzes, a brief profile of the state of Tamil Nadu and that of Chennai city where the study has been done becomes inevitable.

SCENARIO OF TAMIL NADU

Tamil Nadu has an area of 1,30,058 sq.kms. with the population of 6,24,05,679 according to 2001 Census. In the last two decades, there has been a phenomenal growth in the Credit Card Base Sector. Geographical expansion and liberal credit extension were the hallmark of growth phases.

Being the eleventh largest state, Tamil Nadu has been a pioneering state in e-governance initiatives in India, thereby improving the quality of service and transparency in operations. It is the sixth most populous state. 43.86% live in urban areas accounting for 6% of India's population and 9.6% of urban population. Tamil Nadu is the most urbanized state in the country, according to a World Bank study on urbanization in India. Almost 44% of the state is urbanized. The country's urban population which was mere than 288 million in 2002, will nearly double to touch 500 million by 2017. Though a less than a third of the country's population lived in urban areas, they generated two thirds of its gross domestic product (GDP) and almost 90% of the government revenues[1].

Tamil Nadu is the second most industrialized state. Globalization brought increased opportunities making it the fifth largest economy among the states of India. In terms of attracting funds too, T.N. ranks second, next only to U.P., ahead of even the state of Maharashtra (which is popular for its industrialization and trade). World Bank (WB) approved $ 3.8 billion to India in the financial year 2006-2007, a 170% increase over previous years. In terms of commitments by location, U.P. gained 18% followed by Tamil Nadu at 12% and Maharashtra 7%[2].

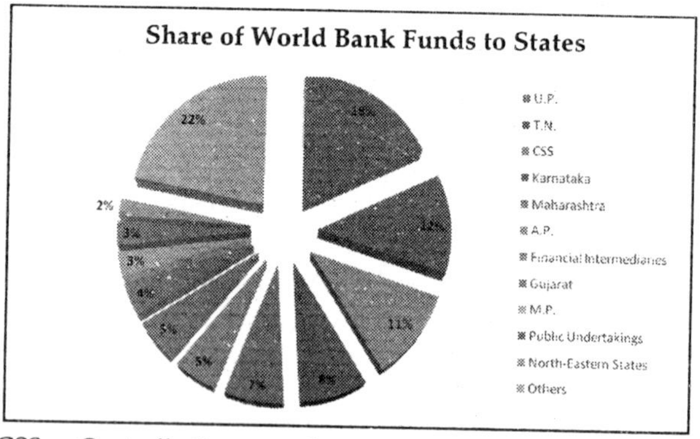

CSS = Centrally Sponsored Schemes

Figure 1

Chennai City–A Profile

Chennai (until 1996, called Madras), the capital city of Tamil Nadu, is one of the leading financial centers in India and ranks among the four major metropolitan and cosmopolitan cities in India. It has a total population of 4,352,932 (4.2 million), as per 2001 census of Tamil Nadu, now estimated to be 7.06 million as of July 2007. The total metropolitan population accounts to 6.4 million which was estimated to grow to 7.6 million by 2006 end and is estimated to reach 8.63 million by 2007 end. Population density in Chennai is 24,418 per sq.km. and that of metropolitan is 5,847 per sq.km. Average literacy rate is 80.14%, much higher than the national average of 59.5%. Chennai is a 368 year old city and is the 34th largest metropolitan area in the world. Chennai is among the densest cities in the world in terms of population per area. The sex ratio is 948 females for every 1000 males. It has the fourth largest *Gross Metropolitan Product* in India. Chennai city has been rated recently as having the highest quality of life among Indian cities. According to a 2007 worldwide quality of life survey done by Mercer, Chennai received the second highest rating in India, first being New Delhi, the capital city of our country. However, it came in at a relatively low 177th worldwide due to poor health and sanitation and increasing air pollution.

Chennai, called the *Gateway to South India,* has emerged as the topper among Indian cities ahead of other three metros (Mumbai, Delhi and Kolkata) as well as Bangalore, based on the *"Location Ranking Survey'* conducted by ECA International. Chennai has improved its global ranking to 138 in 2006-07 from 179 in 2002-03. It is now ranked at 26th position in Asia, in terms of livability, up from 31st rank in 2002-03.

Chennai is the fourth largest city of India and third largest commercial and industrial centre in India. It is also an important centre for banking and finance. At present, it is home to three large level commercial banks and many state-level co-operative banks. Many Indian banks, multinational banks and World Bank have located their back office operations in the city. Hence, Chennai, with its growing popularity has earned the nickname of *"Detroit of South Asia"*.

CURRENT TREND IN CHENNAI CITY

Fifteen to twenty years ago, Chennai was considered to be a *'Conservative'* city when compared to other major cities of India.

In view point of market, it was a Seller's Market. Customers had to buy what was available. Now, with *'Dynamism'* overtaking *'Conservatism'*, and with plenty of choice, it is now a *Buyer's Market*. Technological changes have helped the boom in the industry. People are exposed to western lifestyle and there is a drastic shift in their taste and preferences. Unlike the older generations where the adults were the deciding authorities, the young, dynamic, buoyant current generation keep themselves abreast of the technological changes and the latest trends in the market.

Chennai is considered the *"Retail King of India"*. There is lot of concentration on Chennai market, be it the Indian goods and services or MNC's. Here, the customers take informed decisions after a lot of survey and analysis before buying a product. Urbanization has further led to the concentration of many aspects in this city. As per the Census of India, 2001, the annual growth rate of urban population is 3.56 when compared to 1.79 in 1991 and the Decadal Growth rate has been 42.79 (1991-2001) when compared to 19.59 (1981-1991).

CHENNAI CITY AND CREDIT CARD CULTURE

Credit Card culture is fast catching up in this city. Many payments have begun to be in the mode of credit cards. There is a vast potential in this city, which is yet to be tapped fully.

In Chennai, among the commercial banks, Central Bank of India launched its card in 1980, followed by Andhra Bank in 1981. Bank of Baroda, Canara Bank, Bank of India, State Bank of India, Indian Overseas Bank and Vijaya Bank soon followed suit with other banks like Punjab & Sind Bank, Bank of Madura, Karur Vysya Bank entering the arena. Later, Karur Vysya Bank turned its direction towards debit cards alone.

Citibank, HSBC were the part played by foreign banks in the city. HDFC, ICICI etc. are the latest private Indian banks, but least to say, top among all banks in handling credit card segment.

Among the Indian Banks, Canara Bank and Andhra Bank were the forerunners in Credit Card business. Andhra

Bank Card was the first Indian bank credit card with international affiliation of *VISA* and *Master Card*. It was the first bank in the city which had a computer link with *VISA INTERNATIONAL*.

Perceived initially as an exclusive service for the exclusive elite, the credit card business was, at the beginning, growing slowly, till mid-1987, when suddenly it started booming, with both in the number of issuers as well as credit card holders in the city. The NEP of 1991, added momentum to the already begun boom. Outstanding credit with a credit card company is no longer viewed as a taboo by the people of Chennai city. Possessing a credit card or two is no longer a status symbol. With the process of economic liberalization, the market in Chennai has grown by 25% in the last few years.

"Consumers demand functionality. They only demand a technology when it provides the only means to satisfy a need" – *JOSEPH NAUJOKAS*[3]. Thus with the advent of NEP 1991, technology has given a helping hand to satisfy the demands of the consumers to satisfy their needs in various forms and one form is the credit card culture which has influenced the Chennai city people too.

To know the consumption pattern of spending through credit cards by the customers, their age group, education, income, profession, usage of credit card, their attitude towards usage of debit card per se with credit card etc. have all been taken into consideration, each of which has been analyzed as follows.

DESCRIPTION STATISTICS FOR CUSTOMER SAMPLE

Frequency Distribution and percentage calculation is used to process the data obtained through questionnaire (Enclosure: Annexure IA)

In the second part of the questionnaire, which tries to draw the Behavioural pattern, attitude and the satisfactory level etc. of the respondents possessing credit card(s), apart from the percentage count, mean values also has been computed coupled with rankings to know exactly the purpose of holding a credit card by the consumers.

Table 1
Frequency Distribution of Age Group of Consumers

Age Group (Years)	*Frequency*	*Percentage*
< or = 30	38	25.33
31–40	66	44.00
41–50	30	20.00
Above 50	16	10.67

Source: Collected by researcher by personal investigation

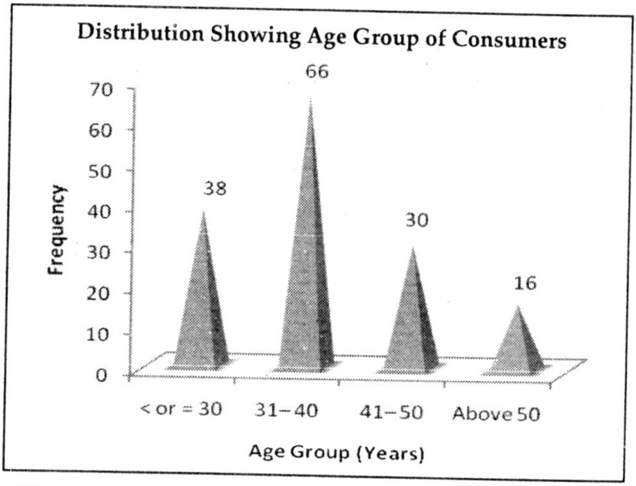

Figure 2: Distribution Showing Age Group of Consumers

Table 1 and Figure 2 shows that age group forms the vital factor under which falls the maximum usage of credit card.. The age group between 31–40 forms the prime age group of consumers to earn and yearn to lead a comfortable life. Following this group is the young, dynamic, aspiring age group who have just started earning or looking out for a good opportunity to settle well in life. Then comes the 40–50 years age group, who by now, have been stabilized and start thinking about the future, followed by the 51 and above age group, who basically want to secure their life as, very shortly they will be entering the retirement age.

Thus, we find that the above analysis correlates very closely to the *Life Cycle Hypothesis* of Ando and Modigliani, wherein the consumption pattern depends upon the availability of resources of the individual consumer, wherein the former peaks during his prime earning time and falls as they near the end period of their lives.

Table 2

Frequency Distribution of the Occupational Pattern of Consumers

Occupation	*Frequency*	*Percentage*
Professional	38	25.33
Employees	82	54.67
Business	12	8.00
Others	18	12.00
Total	150	100.00

Source: Collected by researcher by personal investigation

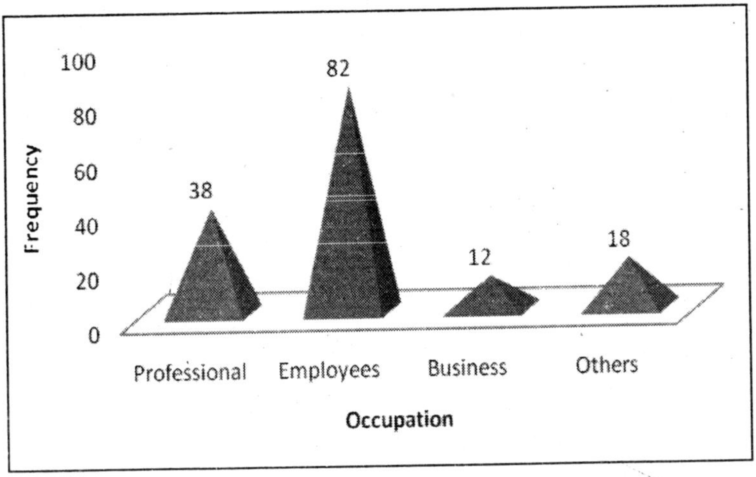

Figure 3: Distribution Showing Occupational Pattern of Consumers

Table 2 and Figure 3 shows the frequency distribution of the occupational pattern of the consumers of the different categories; employees include those employed in the government sector, private sector, labourers of all kinds, and Others include housewives, students, dependants and those who are in the service sector. To the professional category belong the doctors, engineers and the like who do not form part of government employees.

It can be seen that it is the *Employees* category, who form the working, monthly income group, swipe their credit cards the most as it forms 54.67%, followed by the professionals which is 25.33%. 12% consisting of housewives, students and service sector like the ones working in banks, transportation segment, courier offices, postal services etc. forms the third major share while the business people hold a much lesser share of only 8% as many of their transactions are by cash and for business purpose transactions, a safer method via banking operations is opted for.

Table 3
Frequency Distribution of Educational Qualification of Customers

Educational Qualification	*Frequency*	*Percentage*
Up to Higher Secondary	14	9.33
Under Graduation	43	28.67
Post Graduation and above	55	36.67
Professional	38	25.33
Total	150	100.00

Source: Collected by researcher by personal investigation

Tables 2, 3 and Figure 4 show a clear relation between educational qualification and occupation. In real life, we see that higher the education level, more towards earning capacity

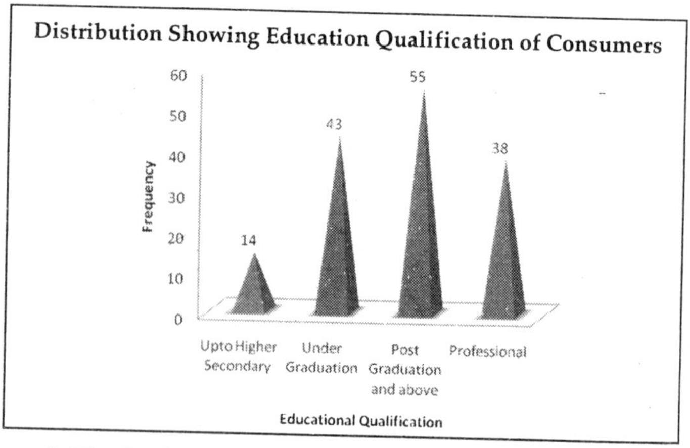

Figure 4: Distribution Showing Educational Qualification of Consumers

which go to form the monthly earning group in the 3 stages of higher, upper middle and middle income groups . Thus we can club under graduation and post graduation groups into one and say that 65.34% form the employee group, followed by the professionals in both the tables while lower level education corresponds to lower levels of monthly income (or income in general), thereby very low level usage of credit cards or add-on cards by the consumers.

Table 4
Frequency Distribution of Monthly Income of Consumers

Monthly Income(In Rupees)	*Frequency*	*Percentage*
< or = 15,000	48	32.00
15,001 – 30,000	39	26.00
30,001 – 45,000	37	24.67
Above 45,001	26	17.33
Total	150	100.00

Source: Collected by researcher by personal investigation

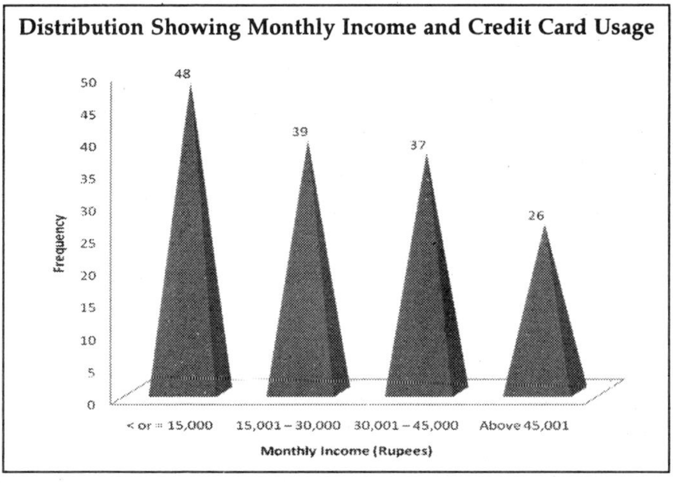

Figure 5: Distribution Showing Monthly Income and Credit Card Usage

Table 4 and Figure 5 shows that when consumers start their independent life, i.e., when they start earning, they aspire and desire to achieve a lot with their earnings. This is further intuited by the mode of living they want to have when they see many people with better earnings than themselves, leading a much more comfortable life. This is alike to the *Demonstration Effect* of Deusenberry, wherein we see that at lesser incomes more people use their credit cards the most while it is vice versa in terms of percentage as income increases, as at higher levels, most of their basic wants are satisfied. This is the period which begins with *Conspicuous Consumption.*

We also see a relation between age group and income levels, though indirectly, since to satisfy their wants, people want to earn a lot, which obviously happens at the age between 20 and 40, in general. Here exceptional cases are not considered. Many settle at their highest earning capacity of their life in the early stages of 40, which is almost like a saturation point, and further increase in their income may not come in at short intervals.

Again, when this point is reached, people cut down on their expenses and want to save for their future life, for the fear of old age, sickness, security of life etc. This again holds a strong relation with the age group Table of 1.

Table 5

Frequency Distribution of Control of Credit Card Expenses in a Family

Control of Credit Card Expenses by the Head Card Holder	*Frequency*	*Percentage*
Yes	83	55.33
No	20	13.33
Take decision together	22	14.67
Not Applicable	25	16.67
Total	150	100.00

Source: Collected by researcher by personal investigation

Table 5 shows that though a credit card in the hands of a consumer means extended freedom of expenditure by him/ her, in reality, there is a visible control on the other members of a family holding a credit card or an add-on card, because–

(a) Many are not happy with the service charges that they pay for every swipe they make.

(b) Probably, credit card expenses dent on their monthly savings which is clear from the set of attitude statements in the questionnaire.

(c) Consumers feel the pinch of credit card expenses when it comes to repayment.

(d) If they go on for roll on payment, then, in due course of time, the interest paid will be equal or greater than the expenditure actually made by a credit card or an add-on card.

(e) Consumers are more rational while expending with their credit cards; education gives them more knowledge of its proper utilization.

Table 6
Frequency Distribution of Preference of Cards by the Consumer

Type of Card	*Frequency*	*Percentage*
Credit	49	32.67
Debit	34	22.67
Both	67	44.67
Total	150	100.00

Source: Collected by researcher by personal investigation.

Table 6 shows that credit card holders are more than debit card holders which shows that credit card usage are definitely on the rise. Another factor attributing to this fact may be that the young age group is more than the old age group comparatively in Chennai. However, it should also be remembered that the table shows that 44.67% have opted for using either a credit or a debit card which means that they do have an eye on their budget, savings and future plans and hence the growing importance of debit cards which gives an immediate impact than credit cards, which has a slow impact on the customers, cannot be ruled out. This higher percentage of using both credit and debit cards (44.67%) than the percentage of credit cards alone (32.67%) may also contribute to the fact that as age and income grows, people satiate their wants and the utility value of credit cards enters the stage of *Diminishing Returns*.

Table 7(a)
Frequency Distribution Showing the Pattern of Usage of Credit Cards by the Consumers

	Yes		*No*		*Preference*			
Items	*Respondent*	*%*	*Respondent*	*%*	*Respondent*	*Total*	*Mean*	*Rank*
Grocery	71	47.33	79	52.67	70	150	**3.49**	**02**
Jewellery	51	34.00	99	66.00	52	150	5.42	11
Entertainment	51	34.00	99	66.00	49	150	5.29	10
Education/Books	53	35.33	97	64.67	54	150	5.85	15
All types of household goods & other utilities	70	46.67	80	53.33	67	150	4.28	07
Tax	10	6.67	140	93.33	12	150	5.67	12
Consumer Durables	73	48.67	77	51.33	73	150	**4.22**	**05**
On-line transactions	44	29.33	106	70.67	45	150	5.16	09
Railway bookings	76	50.67	74	49.33	72	150	4.24	06
Airlines booking	65	43.33	85	56.67	63	150	4.33	08
Clothes	71	47.33	79	52.67	69	150	**3.87**	**03**
Fuel (Petrol, Diesel)	82	54.67	68	45.33	85	150	**2.64**	**01**
Hotels & Restaurants	103	68.67	47	31.33	96	150	**4.20**	**04**
Hospital & Pharmacy	50	33.33	100	66.67	52	150	5.69	13
Various types of loans	9	6.00	141	94.00	15	150	5.80	14

Source: Collected by researcher by personal investigation.

Table 7(a) shows the pattern of usage of credit cards on various items by the consumers and their priority has been calculated and ranked by the researcher. It should be made clear here that according to the changing lifestyles, products available in the market has also undergone a sea change and there are lots of one stop shop stores to make availability of almost everything, if possible, under one roof. This is one way of business technique adopted so as to bind the customer of his purchase in one place. Also the customer is happy since he need not run from one shop to another for every other purchase. Hence the term Grocery is not limited to the strictest sense of its term as it meant a few years before, restricting itself to food items alone. Lot of other items like soaps, shampoos, ready to eat items, soft drinks, juices, shaving kit for the men, party items like disposable cups, papers etc., toiletries and cosmetics etc., too come under this head. The consumer generally makes all these types of monthly purchases also, along with the regular grocery items. This has attributed to the main factor of Grocery acquiring the second rank in terms of preferences as shown in table 7 (b). Similarly fuel applies to fuel filled by consumers on to their vehicles they use, a two wheeler or a four wheeler, and hence only to the petrol or the diesel aspects. The household utilities include the non-recurring or recurring in the long run like the fans, chandeliers to decorate the houses, decorative lights, kitchen utilities like the oven, toaster, mixer-grinder, grinder and the like.

Tables 7(a) and 7(b) shows how much percentage of people opt for various kinds of expenditures through their credit cards and the *Preference* shows the highest level of usage of credit cards by the customers on various aspects. It is clear that *Fuel* and *Grocery* has taken the first and the second place respectively, a crystal clear example of upcoming middle-class behavioural pattern when their sources of income increase. Next few important ranks have been occupied by *Clothes* and *Hotels & Restaurants* expenditures followed by expenses on *Consumer Durables*.

It is also clear that tax occupies only the twelfth position and various types of loans, fourteenth position, which is a direct reflection of savings pattern with banks since these two come under the direct purview of banks' accounts if done through credit cards, thereby showing the national level savings pattern. This is in sharp contrast to developed countries wherein many swipe their credit cards for tax payment, which augurs for more efficient allocation of resources.

Table 7(b)
Mean Values of the Preferences and the Ranks on Various Items

Items	*Mean*	*Rank*
Fuel (Petrol, Diesel)	2.64	01
Grocery	3.49	02
Clothes	3.87	03
Hotels & Restaurants	4.20	04
Consumer Durables	4.22	05
Railway bookings	4.24	06
All types of household goods & other utilities	4.28	07
Airlines booking	4.33	08
On-line transactions	5.16	09
Entertainment	5.29	10
Jewellery	5.42	11
Tax	5.67	12
Hospital & Pharmacy	5.69	13
Various types of loans	5.80	14
Education/Books	5.85	15

Source: Collected by researcher by personal investigation.

Table 8
Frequency Distribution of Superiority of Credit Cards Over Cash Transactions

	Yes		*No*		
Opinion on Usage of Credit Cards	*Respon-dents*	*Percen-tage*	*Respon-dents*	*Percen-tage*	*Total*
Easy to carry	56	37.33	94	62.67	150
Safe	43	28.67	107	71.33	150
Comfortable transaction	78	52.00	72	48.00	150
No difference	8	5.33	142	94.67	150

Source: Collected by researcher by personal investigation.

Table 8 shows the frequency distribution of superiority of credit cards over cash transactions. While 52% have opted for comfortable transaction for credit cards than cash, it can be said that credit cards does have some superiority over cash, not only while transacting for a particular good or service but also helps consumers in increasing their purchasing power with a swipe which may otherwise would make them think twice or impossible due to lack of sufficient cash in hand, if they had to go in for cash transactions. Thus for bridging the immediate want of cash, credit cards come handy to many.

However, it may also be noted that 71.33% are of the view that it is not safe which means that, if a card is lost, it can be fraudulently used by miscreants, which might turn out to be more disastrous than cash loss since, in the latter, it is limited only up to the limit lost, whereas in the former, if a particular credit card has a high value of creditability, the loss occurred may be huge, coupled with the fact that it might have to be paid by the legal credit card holder though he has not swiped it. Thus the importance of *Consumer Protectionism* and the rate of consumer awareness play a vital role here.

Table 9
Frequency Distribution Depicting the Number of Times a Credit Card is Used by Consumers

Frequency in Using Credit Cards	*Frequency*	*Percentage*
Very frequent	24	16.00
Frequent	69	46.00
Rarely	35	23.33
Never	22.5	14.67

Source: Collected by researcher by personal investigation.

Table 9 and the corresponding *figure 6* shows that 46% of the respondents use their credit cards frequently, 16% use very frequently while 23.33% use rarely. Almost 85% of the respondents use their credit cards while only the degree of usage differs. This shows that some consumers want to *Maximize* (frequent users) while some want to *Optimize* (very frequent users on one hand and rare users on the other extreme) their desires for which credit cards come to their help. They try to reach a higher level of satisfaction and welfare through credit cards.

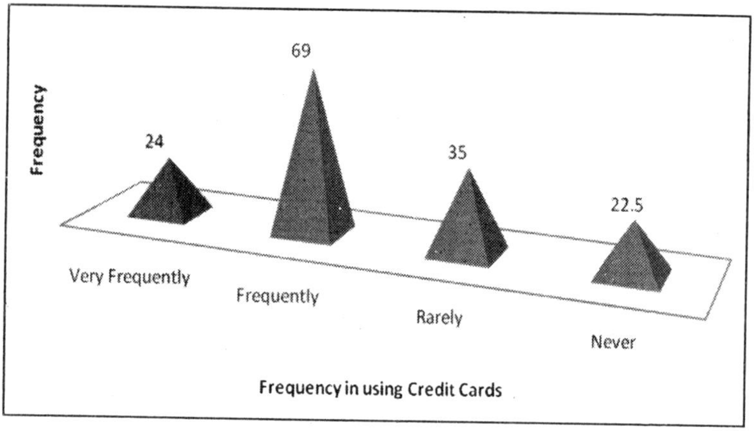

Figure 6: Distribution Depicting the Number of Times a Credit Card is Used by Consumers

Having obtained the basic underlying facts in the first part of the questionnaire, the second part has dealt with reasons for the possession of credit card by the respondents. The reasons were listed and the respondents were asked to tick mark their choice based on their agreement or disagreement with the statements listed in the questionnaire.

The questionnaire has been attached as Annexure IA.

This part deals with inferences that could be made. These are in statement pattern based on Likert Scale of 5 points, varying in different degrees of agreement by various consumers. The different statements of the questionnaire are numbered from S1 to S21 and the mean values thus obtained are as follows based on which ranks are given.

Table 10 shows the mean values of statements for possession of credit cards by the respondents and the mean values and rankings has been calculated by the researcher. The above statements are given in abbreviated form, keeping in tact the meaning, with respect to its appearance in the questionnaire, which contains more detailed sentences.

The first three ranks show the superiority of holding a credit card which is considered better to cash carrying; giving the consumers a boost of confidence as it also helps in times of urgency and emergency which acts as a tremendous substitute for cash. The last two ranks show that consumers are aware of their expenditure pattern to a very large extent and also to a certain extent about the terms and conditions of using a credit card since a roll-on payment would mean increased interest payment for the balance amount. This again means a dent on their savings. Moreover, a credit card is less frequently used by consumers for withdrawal of money from ATM (rank 21) which would mean having a tab on their savings level. Rank 04 highlights the fact that people are willing for more transparency of their transactions if introduced in various segments of payments. This is a healthy feature, not only to the consumers but to the economy as a whole since more transparency would mean more efficiency and plugging off black money circulation in the economy in general.

Table 10
Mean Values of the Statements for Possession of Credit Card and their Rankings

Sl. No.	*Statements*	*Mean*	*Rank*
S1	It gives a social privilege	3.23	13
S2	Better substitute to cash	3.99	01
S3	Increased purchasing power	3.17	15
S4	Helps to lead a comfortable life	2.96	18
S5	Willing to use for lesser amounts too	2.96	18
S6	Make use of multiple cards	3.05	17
S7	Increase in expenditure pattern	3.23	13
S8	Better features to cash	3.49	10
S9	Enough time to mobilize money	3.55	06
S10	Make use of roll over facility	2.65	20
S11	Use frequently at ATMs	2.27	21
S12	Tension free of bank timings	3.54	07
S13	More transparency of expenses	3.54	07
S14	Gives me confidence	3.92	02
S15	Possibility of usage in all situations	3.67	04
S16	Feel the pinch while repaying	3.11	16
S17	Burden of exchange rates abroad	3.49	10
S18	High rate of service charges	3.63	05
S19	Savings unaffected	3.46	12
S20	Use more during emergency	3.76	03
S21	It is a boon	3.52	09

Source: Collected and computed by researcher through personal investigation.

INFERENTIAL STATISTICS ON CUSTOMER SAMPLE FACTOR ANALYSIS

Factor Analysis is a statistical procedure used to uncover relationships among variables. This allows numerous variables to be condensed into fewer dimensions called factors.

In the context of this study, the variables are the degrees of agreement with various specific patterns for holding a credit card by the respondents and the factors are the general underlying patterns.

The method of factor analysis has been adopted in the study to distinguish the relationship between various patterns that go to say the impact of possessing a credit card by the respondents and their perception of holding it from different angles.

The various statements have been sub-divided into various factors by grouping statements of similarity into a single group based on which *Factor Analysis* has been computed. The 5 sets of factors are as follows:

FACTOR 1: BEHAVIOURAL PATTERN

It is a better substitute for cash	S2
Willingness to swipe a credit card even for lesser amounts	S5
It possesses better features than cash	S8
More transparency through statements	S13
Confidence while holding a credit card	S14
Introduction in various segments for its usage	S15
Unaffected monthly budget and savings	S19
It is a boon	S21

FACTOR 2: ATTITUDE

Possessing a credit card as a social privilege	S1
Purchasing increased power	S3
Helps to lead a comfortable life	S4
In case of multiple card possession, use them instead of cash	S6
Expansion in expenditure pattern	S7
Effective usage of roll-over payment system	S10

FACTOR 3: RATIONALITY

Feel the pinch of credit card when it comes to repayment S16
Feel the burden of exchange rates S17
Can be put to more use if interest rates reduced S18

FACTOR 4: CONSUMER SATISFACTION

Arrangement of repayment without affecting savings S9
Frequency in using credit cards for withdrawals from ATMs S11

FACTOR 5: UTILITY VALUE

Tension free of bank timings and bank holidays S12
Use more in times of emergency S20

FINAL STATISTICS: extraction 1 for analysis [Principal Components Analysis PC)].

Table 11
Principal Components Analysis of Consumer Sample

Factor	*Eigen Value*	*Pct of Variable*	*Cumulative Percent*
1	6.659	31.7	31.7
2	1.919	9.1	40.9
3	1.440	6.9	47.7
4	1.171	5.6	53.3
5	1.008	4.8	58.1

Source: Computed by researcher from the collected data.

(VARIMAX rotation 1 for extraction 1 in analysis 1 – Kaiser Normalization. Varimax covered in 9 iterations).

Table 12
Rotated Factor Matrix for Consumer Sample

Factor	*Variable*	*Factor score*
Behavioural pattern	S2	0.727
	S5	0.526
	S8	0.653
	S13	0.648

Contd.

Factor	*Variable*	*Factor score*
	S14	0.699
	S15	0.683
	S19	0.678
	S21	0.669
Attitude	S1	0.699
	S3	0.691
	S4	0.564
	S6	0.584
	S7	0.586
	S10	0.658
Rationality	S16	0.745
	S17	0.493
	S18	0.649
Consumer Satisfaction	S9	-0.535
	S11	0.696
UtilityValue	S12	0.579
	S20	0.575

Source: Computed by researcher from the collected data.

Interpretation of Factor Analysis

The output of factor analysis is obtained through Principal Component Analysis and Varimax Rotation. There are two stages in factor analysis. Stage one being the factor extraction process, wherein the objective is to identify how many factors are to be extracted from the data. The most popular method for this is called the Principal Component Analysis. The higher the Eigen Value of a factor, the higher is the amount of variance explained by the factor.

As evident from *table 11* (looking at Cumulative Per cent Column), we find that the five factors extracted together account for 58.1% of total variance. Hence the numbers of variables have been reduced from twenty one (21) to five (5) above said variables, viz, *Behavioural Pattern, Attitude, Rationality, Consumer Satisfaction* and *Utility Value.*

From *Table 12* we see that S2 have loadings of 0.727, S14 (0.699), S15 (0.683), S19 (0.678), S21 (0.669), S13 (0.648) and S5 (01.526) on Factor 1. This suggests that Factor 1 is a combination of these variables. Therefore, this factor can be interpreted as *"Behavioural Pattern"* of the consumer. Of these S2 has the highest loading which states that people prefer credit cards to cash as it is a better substitute to cash.

Similarly, it is seen that S1 have loadings of 0.699, S3 (0.691), S10 (0.658), S7(0.586), S6(0.584) and S4(0.564) on Factor 2 which is a combination of these variables. Therefore this factor can be interpreted as *"Attitude"* of the consumer towards using a credit card. Of these, S1 has the highest loading which says that possessing a credit card gives social privilege to consumers.

Likewise, Factor 3 has combinations of S16 (0.745), S18 (0.649), S17 (0.493). Factor 4 is a combination of S11 (0.696) and *S9 (-0.535)*. However, S9 has a negative loading on this factor which shows the inverse relationship of the variable in question i.e., consumers find it difficult to arrange for their repayment without affecting their savings level for expenditures met with Credit Cards. This thus happens to be a strong criterion since it leads to the conclusion that there is *Spending Spree* due to Credit Cards, which affects the individuals' savings and thereby national savings and hence national investment (if taken at the national level considering the national credit card spends).

Factor 5 has combinations of S12 with loadings 0.579 and S20 with loadings of 0.575 and come under *Utility Value* variable.

Table 13
Mean and Standard Deviation of Various Factors

Factor Variable	*Mean*	*Sd*
Behavioural Pattern	28.54	6.06
Attitude	15.05	4.38
Rationality	10.23	2.32
Consumer satisfaction	5.82	1.52
Utility Value	7.30	1.69
Overall Opinion about credit card usage	66.95	12.34

Source: Computed by researcher from collected data

Table 13 shows that consumer's Behavioural Pattern has the highest mean of 28.54 followed by their Attitude with 15.05 which shows how the expenditure pattern is biased towards credit card due to possession of them. However, Consumer Satisfaction shows the least mean of 5.82, which means that consumers do face certain problems in holding a credit card which might be contributed by hesitant merchant acceptance due to high service charges, by banks due to penalty of late payment or high roll on interest or by the consumer himself who is rifted by conspicuous consumption.

ANOVA

ANOVA has been used to understand the significant difference between various factors with respect to different variables.

Hypothesis 1

Null hypothesis: There is no significant difference between age group with respect to impact of credit card usage

Table 14
Association Between Age and Credit Card Usage

	Age Group (Mean Values)					
Impact of Credit Card Usage	*< = 30*	*31–40*	*41–50*	*>50*	*F value*	*P Value*
Behavioural pattern	28.29	29.38	26.47	29.56	1.793	0.151
Attitude	16.32	15.03	13.80	14.50	1.995	0.117
Rationality	10.21	10.62	9.43	10.19	1.836	0.143
Consumer satisfaction	5.89	5.74	5.70	6.19	0.454	0.715
Utility value	7.05	7.39	7.30	7.50	0.411	0.745
Overall Opinion	67.76	68.17	62.70	67.94	1.504	0.216

Source: Computed by researcher from collected data.
Note: Values with * denote significance at 5% level (i.e. 0 – 0.01)
Values with ** denote significance at 1% level (i.e. 0.011 to 0.05).
Other values denote greater than 0.05
F-value: Tabulated value
P-value: Computed value

Table 14 shows that all P-values are greater than 0.05. Hence we accept the null hypothesis that there is no significant difference between age groups in using credit cards and reject the alternate hypothesis that Credit Cards have an impact on different age groups. The mean value, though is more (29.56) in the age group greater than 50 for Behavioural Pattern factor and for less than or equal to 30 age group in Attitude (16.32),

31 – 40 age group in Rationality (10.62), in general they all have very small or insignificant contribution in affecting independent factors. Moreover, it can also be viewed in the angle that financial, banking and economic reforms has had an equal impact on all ages which has tempted many to use credit cards.

Hypothesis 2

Null hypothesis: There is no significant difference between occupation with respect to impact of credit card usage.

Table 15
Association between occupation and Credit Card Usage

Impact of Credit Card Usage	*Occupation (Mean Values)*					
	Professional	*Employees*	*Business*	*Others*	*F value*	*P value*
Behavioural pattern	29.03	28.90	26.25	27.39	0.966	0.411
Attitude	14.84	15.43	13.42	14.89	0.792	0.500
Rationality	10.76	10.23	8.83	10.86	2.202	0.090
Consumer satisfaction	5.47	5.95	6.00	2.09	0.911	0.437
Utility value	7.24	7.40	6.92	1.68	0.334	0.081
Overall opinion	67.34	67.91	61.42	65.39	1.081	0.359

Source: Computed by researcher from collected data.

Table 15 shows that since all independent factors and the overall impact is greater than 0.05, we accept the null hypothesis 2 and state that consumers with different types of occupation prefer using credit cards. However, individual mean value for Professionals is the highest in terms of consumer Behavioural pattern (29.03) while that of Consumer Satisfaction is the highest for the businessmen (6.00). On the contrary we find that utility value is the lowest for others group which form the students, housewives (1.68), which means either their usage of credit cards or add on cards are very minimal or nil, as the case may be.

Hypothesis 3

Null hypothesis: There is no significant difference between educational qualifications with respect to impact of credit card usage.

Table 16
Association Between Educational Qualification and Credit Card Usage

	Educational Qualification (Mean Values)					
Impact of Credit Card Usage	*Up to HSc*	*UG*	*PG & above*	*Profes-sional*	*F Value*	*P Value*
Behavioural pattern	28.93	29.21	27.24	29.53	1.312	0.273
Attitude	15.64	15.47	15.05	14.37	0.152	0.859
Rationality	9.43	10.12	10.25	10.63	0.679	0.508
Consumer satisfaction	6.29	5.86	5.75	5.71	0.023	0.513
Utility value	7.36	7.30	7.25	7.34	0.023	0.977
Overall Opinion	67.64	67.95	65.55	67.38	0.469	0.626

Source: Computed by researcher from collected data.

Table 16 shows that since all independent and overall values are all greater than 0.05, we accept the null hypothesis that educational qualification not does have an impact on credit card users and all kinds of people are willing to use credit cards.

Hypothesis 4

Null hypothesis: There is no significant difference between monthly income with respect to the impact of credit card usage.

Table 17
Association Between Monthly Income and Credit Card Usage

	Monthly Income (In Rupees)(Mean Values)					
Impact of Credit Card Usage	*< 15000*	*15001- 30000*	*30001 - 45000*	*> 45000l*	*F Value*	*P Value*
Behavioural pattern	27.40	30.56	26.68	30.27	4.138	0.007**
Attitude	15.63	16.23	13.41	14.58	3.194	0.025*
Rationality	9.98	10.90	9.84	10.27	1.636	0.183
Consumer satisfaction	6.04	5.77	5.62	5.77	0.566	0.638
Utility value	7.17	7.92	6.89	7.19	2.725	0.046*
Overall Opinion	66.21	71.38	62.43	68.08	3.644	0.014*

Source: Computed by researcher from collected data.
Note: Values with * denote significance at 5% level (i.e. 0 – 0.01)
Values with ** denote significance at 1% level (i.e. 0.011 to 0.05)
Other values denotes greater than 0.05.

Table 17 shows that since the P-value is less than 0.01 with respect to consumers' Behavioural Pattern, the null hypothesis is rejected at 1% level thereby concluding that there is a significant difference between monthly income and the impact of credit card usage on behavioural pattern.

For factors relating to Attitude, Consumer Satisfaction and Overall Opinion regarding impact of credit card usage, the P-value is less than 0.05 and hence we reject the null hypothesis at 5% significance level and conclude that there is a significant difference between monthly income and the above mentioned factors.

Thus we find that income plays a vital role in handling credit cards by consumers. It is seen that the mean value for utility of possessing credit cards (7.92) is more for those in the income group of Rs. 15001 – Rs. 30,000, which means there are high value users who yearn to live with their Joneses. The Consumer Satisfaction factor is also higher in terms of high mean value in this group which shares its position with the earning group of more than Rs, 45,000/- per month (5.77). However, the level of satisfaction varies in the two groups in the sense, in the former, credit card helps to acquire goods and services to satisfy their highest desire of living with the Joneses, for the latter, who already come under the highly paid group and who would have already fulfilled their materialistic wants of comfortable life, consider possessing credit card as a social privilege which helps them in acquiring more luxury or status.

Hypothesis 5

Null hypothesis: There is no significant difference between type of card owned with respect to impact of credit card usage

Table 18 shows that since the P-value is less than 0.01 for factors relating to Behavioural Pattern (0.0002), Rationality (0.002) Utility Value (0.0002) and in Overall opinion (0.0002) with regard to the impact of credit card usage in relation to the type of card owned (which includes both debit and credit card possessed and used by the consumer), at 1% level, the null hypothesis is rejected. Here, we accept the alternate hypothesis that there is a significant difference between debit and credit cards usage by customers, wherein the mean value is high for customers preferring both (29.24) in the case of consumer behavior, 10.56 in the case of rationality and 7.56 in the case of utility value. However, it should also be noted that there is only a marginal difference between those using both debit and credit cards, while those willing to use credit cards alone, which again means the rising importance of debit cards in the long run usage of both cards. When more debit cards are used, more manipulation on savings and consumption level, the latter tending to reduce. *The increased MPS via debit cards and reduced MPC via credit cards sets in the mind of the consumers.* This is more supported and strengthened when income also starts rising since usage of credit cards by higher income group shows a decline.

Table 18
Association Between Type of Card Owned and Their Usage

	Type of Card Owned (Mean Values)				
Impact of Credit Card Usage	*Credit*	*Debit*	*Both*	*F-value*	*P-value*
Behavioural pattern	28.66	21.10	29.24	9.099	0.0002**
Attitude	15.17	12.40	15.27	1.999	0.139
Rationality	10.00	8.00	10.56	6.193	0.002**
Consumer satisfaction	5.95	4.90	5.86	2.033	0.134
Utility value	7.17	5.30	7.56	9.208	0.0002**
Overall Opinion	66.95	51.70	68.48	9.337	0.0002**

Source: Computed by researcher from collected data.

In other variables, that is, Attitude and Consumer Satisfaction, the P-value is greater than 0.05 and there is no significant difference between the type of card owned and their usage.

STUDENT'S t TEST

This test has been employed in the study to judge the significant difference between the means of two samples.

Hypothesis 6

Null hypothesis: There is no significant distribution between comfortable payments with respect to dimension of credit card usage.

Table 19
Dimension of Credit Card Usage with Respect to its Service Charges

	Comfortable for Paying Service Charges (Mean Values)			
Dimension of Credit Card Usage	*Yes*	*No*	*t value*	*p value*
Behavioural pattern	29.73	27.98	1.66	0.099
Attitude	15.65	14.77	1.14	0.257
Rationality	9.90	10.39	1.22	0.223
Consumer satisfaction	6.19	5.65	2.05	0.042*
Utility value	7.71	7.11	2.06	0.041*
Overall Opinion	69.17	65.90	1.52	0.131

Source: Computed by researcher from collected data.

Table 19 shows that since the P-value is less than 0.05, we reject the null hypothesis at 5% level of significance with regard to Consumer Satisfaction and Utility Value with respect to the impact of credit card usage and payment of service charges for their swiping in every transaction. In other factors, since they are greater than 0.05 at 5% level, we accept the null hypothesis that there is no significant difference between service charge payment and swiping of credit cards.

CHI-SQUARE TEST

This test has been applied to determine whether the data collected shows dependency or the classifications are independent.

Hypothesis 7

Null hypothesis: There is no association between educational qualification and type of card preferred to use.

Table 20 shows that since the P-value is less than 0.05 at 5% significance level, we reject the null hypothesis and accept the alternate hypothesis that education does have an impact on inducing the customers to use more of credit cards. In the above table, we find that the row percentage is highest by professionals who opt to use credit cards (52.56) whereas it is the highest for debit cards in the PG and above group (32.7), which could be contributed by the fact that they could be students or dependents on the earning member.

Table 20
Association Between Education and Preference of Card

	Type of Card Preferred to Use					
Educational Qualification	*Credit*	*Debit*	*Both*	*Row Total*	*Chi-square value*	*P value*
Up to Higher Secondary	7 (50.0)	2 (14.3)	5 (35.7)	14		
UG	10 (23.3)	10 (23.3)	23 (53.5)	43		
PG and above	12 (21.8)	18 (32.7)	25 (45.5)	55	15.968	0.014*
Professional	20 (52.56)	4 (10.5)	14 (36.8)	38		
Column Total	49	34	67	150		

Source: Computed by researcher from collected data.

Education forms the major source of human resource to any country. Greater the impart of education, higher the value of human resource for an economy. Education also imparts knowledge which becomes obvious in one form like increase in the number holding bank account in an economy since they are able to understand the workings of a bank. Hence along with education and banking reforms, improvement in the human resource development paves way for greater economic reforms. One such form is the acceptance of credit cards and its usage which leads to better transparency and efficiency in a country. India, however, lags way behind many countries and has a banking population of just around 20% of the total population, which is a meager figure. Agriculture still being predominant in India though industrialization was advocated much earlier in the times of late Prime Minister Pt. Jawaharlal Nehru, and the invitation to globalization, privatization and liberalization by the then Prime Minister Shri Narasimha Rao under the auspices of the current Prime Minister, Dr. Manmohan Singh (who then was the Finance Minister in Shri.Narasimha Rao's regime), and the contribution to education being approximately around 6% of GDP when compared to other countries, human resource tapping is much at a nascent stage. India has higher untapped potential. With a majority living in rural areas and among the urbanized people, many falling under the lower and middle middle-income group, penetration of banking reforms done in NEP 1991 and the scenario post 1991 has a long way to go. Most of the poor do not have access to the banking system though there are around 67,000 bank branches spread across the country. With many such limitations, Kisan Credit Card (KSC) Scheme was introduced by the Indian Government for the provision of timely and adequate credit to farmers. KSC, though not exactly a credit card in the strict sense of its term, has however, seeded the idea of a credit card system among the Indian farmers too. This has been a major breakthrough, though not a highly celebrated one, by the bankers and the banking sector.

Hypothesis 8

Null hypothesis: There is no association between monthly income and type of card preferred to use.

Table 21
Association Between Monthly Income of Respondents and Preference of Card

	Type of Card Preferred to Use					
Monthly Income (Rs.)	*Credit*	*Debit*	*Both*	*Row Total*	*Chi-square value*	*P value*
< / = 15,000	15 (31.3)	9 (18.8)	24 (50.0)	48		
15,001 - 30,000	12 (30.8)	17 (43.6)	10 (25.6)	39		
31,001 – 45,000	11 (29.7)	6 (16.2)	20 (54.1)	37	16.380	0.012*
> 45,000	11 (32.7)	2 (22.7)	13 (44.7)	26		
Column Total	49	34	67	150		

Source: Computed by researcher from collected data.

Table 21 shows the association between monthly income of respondents and preference of card. It can be seen since the P-value is less than 0.05 at % level, (which is 0.012), we reject the null hypothesis and conclude that there is association between monthly income and type of card preferred to use.

Hypothesis 9

Null hypothesis: There is no significant difference between mean ranks towards preference to use Credit Cards

Table 22
Usage of Credit Cards on Various Item by Respondents

Items	*Mean Rank*	*Chi-Square Value*	*P-Value*
Grocery	8.62		
Jewellery	7.62		
Entertainment	7.62		
Education/ Books	7.72		
All types of Household	8.57		
And other utilities Tax	5.57		
Consumer Durables	8.72		
On-line transactions	7.27	164.318	0.000**
Railway Bookings	8.87		
Airline booking	8.32		
Clothes	8.62		
Fuel	9.17		
Hotels & Restaurants	10.22		
Hospital & Pharmacy	7.57		
Various types of loans	5.52		

Source: Computed by researcher from collected data.

In *Table 22,* the P-value (0.000) is less than 0.01 at 1% significance level and hence we reject the null hypothesis stating that consumers are prepared to swipe their credit cards for any item and accept the fact that *there is preference on various items.* Consumers *Reveal their Preference* to a basket of goods and services available to them.

CORRELATION CO-EFFICIENT

This method has been employed to know the relationship between the various factors that has been sub-divided into statements.

Table 23 shows that the correlation co-efficient between Behavioural Pattern and Attitude is 0.554, almost 55% relationship between these two factors followed by Consumer Satisfaction and Attitude which has 51% relationship. The relationship between Behavioural pattern and Utility Value is 0.494, almost 49 % (marginally less to 50% relationship).

Table 23
Relationship Between Various Factors in Consumer Sample

Totals	*Consumer Behaviour*	*Attitude*	*Rationality*	*Con. Satisfn.*	*Utility Value*
Consumer	1.000	0.554	0.402	0.466	0.494
Behaviour attitude	0.402	1.000	0.377	0.511	0.389
Rationality	0.402	0.378	1.000	0.211	0.395
Con.satisfaction	0.466	0.511	0.211	1.000	0.303
Utility value	0.494	0.389	0.395	0.303	1.000

Source: Collected by researcher by personal investigation.

In all the 'one-to-one factor' cases, all values are positive and hence there is a *Direct Relationship* between the impacts of credit card usage on customers in various walks of life. There is a positive correlation between each factor to every other factor which itself proves that Credit Cards has become part and parcel of consumers' transactions and gives a vivid picture of the growth and potential of credit cards in the near future. Having analyzed the consumers' side, the researcher has analyzed the second side of the coin in a transaction, viz., a detailed view of data collected through merchant questionnaires.

For any transaction to take place, there should be a person to sell the goods and services as per the requirement of the consumer and willing to accept his mode of payment for his sales, else the transaction may not take place and becomes invalidated. Hence, if a consumer produces a credit card as money, the merchant should be willing to accept the same as equivalent to cash and validate the transaction. Thus, his importance enters the picture which has been dealt in detail which forms the second part of the analysis.

MERCHANT QUESTIONNAIRE

Analysis And Interpretation

As a cross-sectional analysis, merchants accepting credit cards were also reviewed. When a transaction takes place, it is between the customer and a merchant and hence it can be considered worthwhile if we are able to cross verify as to how much of the credit cards are being swiped by the customers for various types of transactions, for which merchants' views form a clear reflection.

In order to know the buyers' market in terms of credit card acceptance for their goods and services produced, a sample size of 75 merchants in Chennai city has been taken based on which the following analysis and interpretations are made.

Table 24
Frequency Distribution Showing the Various Types of Merchants in the Market

	Frequency	*Percentage*
Agent/Dealer	13	17.33
Partner	10	13.33
Franchisee	10	13.33
Own Business	42	56.00
Total	75	100.00

Source: Collected by researcher by personal investigation.

Table 24 shows that around 56% of the merchants are having their own business, which would mean accepting a credit card or not can be self-decided without relying on their superiors, as the case may otherwise be. Also, this decision plays a vital role since for every swipe, a telephone call amount is being charged coupled with the service charge which has to be borne either by them for the transaction made or to be levied on the customer, the latter leading to loss of customer in terms of loyalty, if his customer is not happy for the charges levied. If borne by the merchant, whether it affects his profit margin is also a question to be considered, which is analyzed in the latter part of this section.

Table 25
Frequency Distribution Showing the Percentage of Credit Card Acceptance Level

Acceptance Level	*Frequency*	*Percentage*
Yes	68	90.67
No	7	9.33
Total	75	100.00

Source: Collected by researcher by personal investigation.

Table 25 shows that 90.67% accept credit card swiping for purchases made in their shops. This is a direct indication that many customers are willing to pay by credit card and hence in order not to lose their customers and as per the latest trend of shopping, merchants are also willing to accept credit cards as payments. *This shows a Healthy Growth trend of Credit Cards in the market involving Buyers and Sellers.* Also the latest mode of transactions are being made through internet, it shows that while physical presence for a transaction to be undertaken has shrunk, the economic world has widened with more opportunities for all.

Table 26
Frequency Distribution Showing Acceptance of Other Types of Pass (like Sodexho, Ticket Restaurant etc.)

Acceptance of Other Pass	*Frequency*	*Percentage*
Yes	10	13.33
No	65	86.67
Total	75	100.00

Source: Collected by researcher by personal investigation.

Table 26 shows that apart from credit cards, other types of pass which comes as a supplement to cash on purchase of goods and services from merchants, also are in vogue though their percentage is very meager, i.e. only 13.33% whereas acceptance of credit cards has been 90%. However, in future, it cannot be ruled out that, apart from debit card usage which forms a stiff competition to credit card usage since the latter can be immediately collated similar to cash transactions, these passes too, might be on the increase, if people prefer redemption of such passes instead of future payments.

However, it is also worth noting that such passes attract higher service charges than credit card swiping at many merchant establishments, and hence credit cards would definitely be preferred to such passes or redemptions, both, from the point of views of buyers (consumers) and sellers (merchants).

Table 27 and Figure 7 shows that banks, who are the major issuers of credit cards, form the highest percentage, i.e., 58.67%

in approaching merchants to have their terminals, which means easing the job of the customers to use their bank's credit cards. Thus enters the important role of banks in helping the growth rate of credit cards, both from the consumer's side by issuing them the power of this card and on the other hand, by approaching the merchants in installing the point of sale terminals when the customer approaches for transaction on a credit card. POS terminals are a form of *Infrastructure* provided by banks for the potential growth of credit card sector.

Table 27
Frequency Distribution Showing Issuer Choice by Merchants for Pos Terminals

Issuer Choice	*Frequency*	*Percentage*
Bank approached	44	58.67
Self approach	14	18.67
Advertisements	10	13.33
External influence	7	9.33
Total	75	100.00

Source: Collected by researcher by personal investigation.

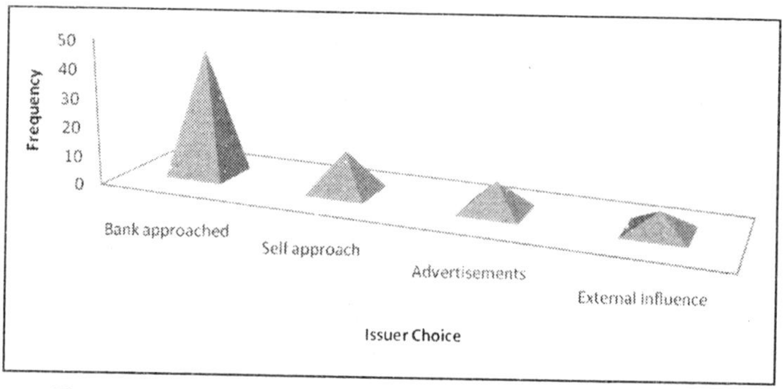

Figure 7: Distribution Showing Issuer Choice by Merchants

Table 28 and Figure 8 clearly specifies that around 57.33% bear the service charges being levied on swiping a credit card. Hence, if banks consider reducing the service charges, merchants would be more forthcoming in accepting credit cards, without loss of loyalty by their customers. It is also clear from the above table that a meager share of just 2.67% is shared between the issuing banks, in sharp contrast to 58.67% being approached by banks to install their terminals for more usage of their bank credit card. It is also worth noting that for 14.67% of merchants, this charge is not applicable, percentage more than the percentage of sharing between bank and merchant with respect to levy of charges. This may be due to the fact that there could be an agreement between the issuing bank and the particular merchant. This way seem to be more effective since neither the customer, nor the merchant, nor does the bank bear the burden of service charge directly, affecting none in the process, which seemingly appears to be a happy situation of credit card usage from all the three perspectives.

Table 28
Frequency Distribution Showing the Burden of Service Charges Borne by Merchants

Issuer Choice	*Frequency*	*Percentage*
Bank	8	10.67
Customer	8	10.67
Merchant (ME)	43	57.33
Shared between ME and Customer	3	4.00
Shared between ME and Bank	2	2.67
Not Applicable	11	14.67
Total	75	100.00

Source: Collected by researcher by personal investigation.

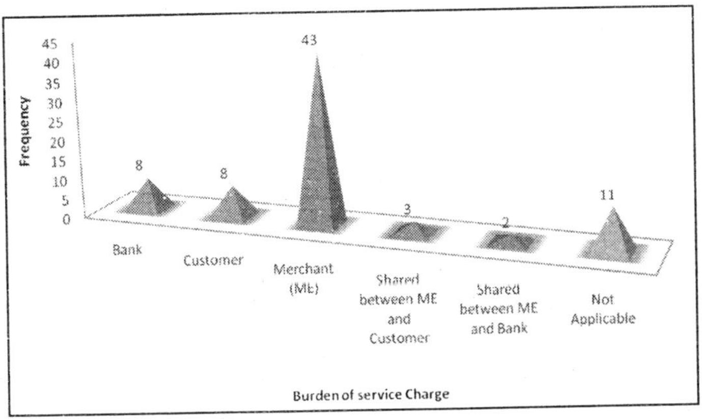

Figure 8: Distribution Showing Burden of Service Charges Borne by Merchants

However, it should also be noted from the table 5.29 and 5.30 below that the percentage of merchants giving special privilege to a particular bank card nor any bank giving special benefits to a particular merchant is also quite low, which means that every credit card transaction is sorted out between the customer and the merchant with least foregoing from either side, *a situation akin to Pareto concept* of optimal usage and acceptance of credit cards by the consumers and merchants, by both trying to be better off without trying to make the other worse off. Otherwise, credit card would not have swept the market with such vigour and force.

Table 29
Frequency Distribution Showing Promotional Scheme Undertaken for a Particular Bank Card

Promotional Scheme	*Frequency*	*Percentage*
Yes	14	18.67
No	61	81.33
Total	75	100.00

Source: Collected by researcher by personal investigation.

Table 30
Frequency Distribution Showing Promotional Activities Undertaken by Merchants for a Particular Bank Card to Increase Sales

Promotional Scheme to Increase Sales	*Frequency*	*Percentage*
Yes	18	24.00
No	57	76.00
Total	75	100.00

Source: Collected by researcher by personal investigation.

The *Second Part* of the questionnaire pertains to understand the penetration of credit cards in the Sellers Market and the comfort level of accepting the same by them. A compare and contrast situation to cash transaction has been tried to arrive at, the extent of credit cards holding a superior position , in a merchant – customer relationship. The minimum transaction cost on the part of the merchant to accept a credit card and the desire to swipe the credit card for the minimum purchase and the possibility of both reaching an *equilibrium transaction* level has been tried to be interpreted and analyzed through these set of statements.

These statements are based on Likert Scale of degree 5, ranging between the most agreeable statement to the most disagreeable statement, depicting their attitude and behavioural pattern, market structure and market trend with respect to penetration of credit cards. There are 16 statements ranging from S1 to S16 and the mean values have been computed which are as follows.

Table 31 shows the mean values and ranking of statements obtained from questionnaires. *Rank 1* shows the highest place that could be occupied by a new invention called the *Plastic Money*, in the form of *Credit Cards*. This new innovation and invention reminds us of the *Schumpeterian Theory of Innovations*, wherein the initial impact of innovation is witnessed by *Rank* 3 in the above table, emphasized more by *Rank 7* which also has a direct bearing on the customers' side who chooses to use credit cards in their initial stages of earnings to achieve certain aspirations in life.

Table 31
Mean Values and Ranks of Statements

Sl. No.	*Statements*	*Rank*	*Mean*
S1	Consumer market is flooded with variety of goods	4.16	2
S2	The innovation and introduction of credit card has come as a boon	4.28	1
S3	No much difference in accepting cash or credit card	3.39	13
S4	People are willing to spend more than before	3.97	3
S5	Sales has increased after beginning to accept credit cards	3.64	10
S6	Able to retain customers by accepting credit cards	3.87	5
S7	Customers are willing to swipe even for lower amounts	3.73	9
S8	Credit card usage more for bulky / large transactions	3.95	4
S9	20 – 45 age group use credit cards the most	3.77	7
S10	Customers are not happy to pay service charge	3.39	13
S11	There is no difference between a credit or a debit card	3.77	7
S12	Comfortable accepting credit cards than cash due to its features	3.41	12
S13	Special benefits accrued for certain bank cards	2.88	16
S14	Accepting credit card does not hinder profit margin	3.21	15
S15	There is an increase in customer base	3.55	11
S16	Expect more credit card transactions in future	3.83	6

Source: Computed by researcher from collected data..

Then follows the *second stage of Schumpeter's Theory* through reactions to the original impact of innovation as seen by *Rank 4* and *Rank 5* from the above table wherein slowly maximum transaction by credit card is replaced by transactions involving bulk amount supported by the fact that as income increases, the percentage of credit card usage decreases (which has already been seen in the customer questionnaire analysis).

INFERENTIAL STATISTICS ON MERCHANT SAMPLE FACTOR ANALYSIS

Like the customers' view, the merchants' view also has been tried to be analyzed by splitting the statements into five sets of factors, each factor organized into a group having similar objectives.

As per table 31, the following statements are clubbed together to form a factor.

Table 32
Principal Components Analysis (PC) of Merchant Sample (Extraction 1)

Factor Percentage	*Eigen Value*	*Percentage of Variance*	*Cumulative Percent*
1	3.332	20.8	20.8
2	1.944	12.1	33.0
3	1.578	9.9	42.8
4	1.377	8.6	51.4
5	1.110	6.9	58.4

Source: Computed by researcher from collected data.

Table 33
Categorization of Different Statements into Variables of Merchant Sample

Statement Numbers	*Factor*	*Variable*
S2, S4, S7, S9, S11, S12	1	Market Structure
S5, S6, S15	2	Market Demand
S1, S8, S16	3	Influence on Sales
S10, S14	4	Rational Behaviour
S3, S13	5	Market Trend

Source: Computed by researcher from collected data.

As evident from *Table* 32 (looking at Cumulative Per cent Column), we find that the five factors extracted together account for 58.4% of total variance. Hence the number of variables has been reduced from 16 to 5 underlying factors.

Table 34
Rotated Factor Matrix

Factor	*Variable*	*Factor Score*
Market Structure	S2	0.538
	S4	0.708
	S7	0.708
	S9	0.436
	S11	0.453
	S12	0.641
Market Demand	S5	0.672
	S6	0.829
	S15	0.063
Influence on Sales	S1	0.749
	S8	0.805
	S16	0.033
Rational	S10	0.779
Behaviour	S14	0.746
Current Market trend	S3	0.758
	S13	0.750

Source: Collected by researcher by personal investigation.

INTERPRETATION OF FACTOR ANALYSIS

Table 32 shows that S4 and S7 have loadings of 0.708 each respectively followed by S12 (0.641), S2 (0.537), S11 (0.453) and S9 (0.436). The values in the brackets show the loading, that is, each variable that has a bearing on the factor. This suggests that Factor 1 is a combination of these variables. Therefore this factor can be interpreted as *"Market Structure"*.

Similarly, variables from statements S6 with loading 0.805, S1 with 0.672 and S15 with 0.063 have been combined to be interpreted as *Market Demand*.

S8 with loading 0.805, S1 with 0.749, and S16 with 0.033 have been combined to form the factor *Influence on Sales*.

S10 with 0.779 and S14 with 0.746 loadings respectively form the factor *Rational Behaviour* of the merchants.

Variables S3 with loading 0.758 and S13 with loading 0.750 have been clubbed to form the factor *"CURRENT MARKET TREND"* of credit card in the sellers' market.

Table 35

Mean Rank of Variables of Merchant Sample

Factor	*Variable*	*Mean Rank*
Consumer market is flooded with various types of goods	S1	10.52
The innovation of credit card is a boon to various groups of people	S2	11.23 (1)
There is no much difference between cash or credit card payment	S3	7.22
People of Chennai city are willing to spend to acquire comfort	S4	9.88
Sales have increased after accepting credit cards	S5	8.17
Able to retain customers by accepting credit card	S6	9.31
Customers are willing to swipe credit cards for lesser amounts	S7	8.69
Credit cards are used for large or bulky purchase	S8	9.50
Age group between 20 – 45 use credit cards the most	S9	8.69
Customers are dissatisfied if they bear the service charges	S10	7.18
There is no difference between a credit or a debit card	S11	8.72
More comfortable accepting credit card than cash	S12	7.30
Our establishment receives special benefits from a particular bank	S13	5.59 (16)
Credit Card acceptance does not hinder our profit margin	S14	6.87
My customer base has increased after accepting credit cards	S15	8.19
In future, expect more credit card payments by customers	S16	8.95

Source: Computed by researcher from collected data.

Table 35 shows the mean rank of variables which in turn depicts the position of the factor in deciding the credit card acceptance by merchants.

The first five rankings and the last ranking are highlighted within brackets. Accordingly, the innovation of credit card stands first in terms of rank which clearly depicts the importance of credit cards, not only among the customers, but also among the merchants to accept them. It is followed by the Market Structure (S1), wherein it is once again clear that supply of various brands and types are available to consumers who has a lot of choice to choose between, which is clearly a BUYERS' MARKET, as per today's trend. Hence any objection raised by a merchant in accepting credit cards will make him lose his customers. This again proves the superiority of credit cards in today's life when compared to other modes of payment, more so by cash. This is further supported by the fact of rank 5 which states that merchants are able to retain their customers by accepting credit cards, which otherwise would mean breach of customer loyalty. "Comfortable living" has become the main motto for many.

Ranks 3 and 4 show that Chennai city is no more a conservative city as it was used to be. The PURCHASING POWER in the hands of the consumers has increased and they are willing to spend more for their comfort.

The last rank, that is, rank 16 states that though merchants' profit margins are affected, the amount and volume of sales, increase in customer base, increased customer loyalty in retaining their customers apart from brand name and reputation earned by them, surpasses the loss encountered by them by bearing the service charges partly or fully, if any, by them. Now they have more sales than before and the sacrifice they make is worth in exchange of accepting credit cards. This is similar to Kaldor-Hicks Welfare criterion which states that there is an increase in social welfare if those who gain from the change could compensate the losers and still better off than before.

All these prove the prowess of credit cards and its gaining popularity and usage in general. Right now, the innovation of credit cards is in the stage of INCREASING RETURNS TO SCALE, since both customer loyalty and customer base have increased, according to the merchants, bringing more revenues through increased sales and thereby more profits leading to more expectations, from the merchants' perspective.

STUDENT'S t-TEST

Hypothesis 10

Null hypothesis: There is no significant difference between acceptance of credit cards and other modes of payment by merchants.

Table 36 shows that since the P-value of acceptance (0.033) is less than 0.05 at 5% significance level, we reject the null hypothesis and conclude that there is a significant difference between acceptance by credit cards and other modes of payment by merchants.

Table 36
Association Between Acceptance of Credit Cards and Other Modes of Payment

Acceptance of Credit Card	*Mean Value*	*SD**	*Total*	*T-value*	*P-value*
Yes	59.353	6.819	68	2.18	0.033*
No	53.429	7.254	7	2.07	0.077

Source: Collected by researcher by personal investigation
* SD = Standard deviation
P-value = Calculated value
T-value = Table value

Hypothesis 11

Null hypothesis: There is no association between the nature of business and credit card acceptance

Table 37
Association Between Nature of Business and Credit Card Acceptance

Type of Business	*Yes*	*No*	*Row Total*	*Chi-square value*	*P-value*
Agent/Dealer	13	–	13		
	(100.0)		(17.3)		
Partner	10	–	10		
	(100.0)		(13.3)		
Franchisee	7	3	10	7.417	0.060
	(70.0)	(30.0)	(13.3)		
Own	38	4	42		
	(9.05)	(9.3)	(56.0)		
Column Total	68	7	75		

Source: Computed by researcher from collected data.

Table 37 shows that since the P-value (0.06) is greater than 0.05 at 5% significance level, we accept the null hypothesis that there is no particular association between nature of business and credit cards acceptance by merchants and conclude, irrespective of the business, all types of merchants accept credit cards for their transactions.

Hence we know that the growth of credit cards has gained high momentum.

Hypothesis 12

Null hypothesis: There is no association between the issuer and acceptance.

Table 38 shows that since the P-value 0.003 is less than 0.05 at 5% significance level, we reject the null hypothesis and conclude that there is a significant association between the issuer of credit card and its terminal by the issuer and acceptance of credit cards from customers by merchants.

Thus, having dealt the merchants' views, the third part of the analysis ventures into the banks' perspectives of issuing credit cards. Be it any form of payment, it should be approved by the government and only the banks have the right, in general, approved by the Central Bank, to float the mode of payment, be it cash, cheque, demand draft etc. The same holds good for credit cards too. Though in other countries NGOs too are in the field of credit cards, as far as India is concerned, till date, only the banks are the issuers of credit cards which is accepted as a mode of payment. Hence it becomes important to know their views too.

BANKS' VIEWS ON FLOATING CREDIT CARDS

Banks form the sole Credit Card Issuers or Acquirers in India and hence their views on the potentiality of credit card growth become inevitable. As stated earlier, though many banks are in operation in Chennai city and many issue or acquire credit cards, the study has been limited only to those banks which have head office in Chennai city or which have a strong back office in Chennai City with respect to credit card segment. Thus the number of banks under survey has been limited. Moreover, there are many agents to a bank to market their bank credit cards. For the study, however, either the Head of the Credit Card Division or Senior Managers related to credit card sector were personally approached for acquiring information through discussion, interview, and their direct opinion in the questionnaire format has been obtained. Major 7 banks from

Table 38
Association Between Issuer of Credit Cards and Merchants

	Row Per cent	*Bank Approached*	*Self Approach*	*Advertise-ment*	*External Influence*	*Row Total*	*Chi- square value*	*P-value*
Yes	1	43	13	6	6	68		
		(63.2)	(19.1)	(8.8)	(8.8)	(90.7)		
No	2	1	1	4	1	7	13.989	0.003
		(14.3)	(14.3)	(57.1)	(14.3)	(9.3)		
Column Total		44	14	10	7	75		
		(58.7)	(18.7)	(13.3)	(9.3)	(100.0)		

Source: Computed by researcher from collected data.

the handful of banks in question were approached for the survey, based on which the analysis has been made. Even though the banks' sample size is very less, it forms the core, since it is the bankers who form the operators, issuers and acquirers of credit cards in India. Also with the inception of various financial sector reforms, credit card has been considered as a major invention, a substitute for money. Since all angles needs to be analyzed, the study has given due importance to banks' views too.

With respect to this particular segment, that is the Credit Card, banks, in general, would like to maintain secrecy with respect to their bank's market share, current trend of their bank's credit cards in the market, future prospects etc. as this industry is a highly potential industry and there is cut-throat competition. Hence for specific questions relating to their bank's credit card segment or credit card holders, a general reasoning alone could be obtained. Many questions were viewed as the general scope of the credit card sector rather to the specific case of the respective bank. Therefore, the analysis made from the bank's point of view is rather a general one based on the common characteristics and the overall phenomena of the total scenario in Chennai City.

This questionnaire too, had two sections. Part I dealt with basic information about the respective bank in relation to credit card sector. Part II was in statement format pertaining to the levels of agreement or disagreement about every statement based on Likert scale of degree 5.

The survey found out that almost all banks agreed that Credit Card segment had taken a giant leap in their retailing sector and their growth constantly and steadily increasing. This fact was also agreed upon in general that the age group between 20 and 45 swiped their respective bank cards the most than the other age groups, and they were also aware of the pinch of service charges borne either by the customers or the merchants, as the case may be. They have increased their customer base considerably after the introduction of their bank's credit cards and that many were either trying to woo the customers or the merchants to increase the swipe of their bank's credit cards, either in the form of loyalties or discounts or any other type, which differed from bank to bank in their approach, for acquiring more market share.

However, the study found out that not much customers are availing the roll-over system, which is not profitable to the banks, a specific requirement to make high profits in the credit card segment. Also for queries relating to credit card debts and frauds the answers obtained were quite sceptical when compared to the roars and cries of many episodes that appear in newspapers, journals and magazines in reality. It is also noteworthy to mention here that not all banks are particular about the qualification or income background while issuing credit cards and more so the add-on cards, as long as they keep receiving the debt amounts regularly. Also tax payment, a transparent account to all – the government, bank and the customer, is not being widely swiped through credit cards by cardholders, which if encouraged to be done, will improve efficiency and transparency of the economy as a whole.

Just to have a contrast study in knowing the growth of credit card sector in the city, Karur Vysya Bank was approached, which are into only debit cards. It should be noted that they were issuers of credit cards initially, mainly co-branding, but later switched to debit cards alone. The reason being that debit cards are safer both from the customer point of view and from the bank's point of view and more than that, they are expecting the growth of debit cards to be higher than credit cards in the future. Though this is *not* in contrast to the views of other banks, the rest are not so doubtful about the future growth of credit cards and feel that both debit and credit card growths are sailing on the same boat, and with changing lifestyles of today's youngsters, credit cards can do wonders.

Despite all the above drawbacks, the banks are confident of improving the performance of the credit card segment, which is highly untapped, and thereby the services rendered by the banks to its customers through credit cards and expect bright prospects of this sector in future.

SUMMARY AND CONCLUSIONS OF THE ANALYSES

To highlight again, the study was conducted in Chennai City by dividing the city into four divisions and the method of purposive random sampling was used with the help of questionnaires. Three sets of distinct survey were conducted for the same dividing the study from the perspectives of the consumers, merchant establishments and the credit card issuing banks.. The study did not segregate the city into urban, semi-urban, rural or any other type and hence the results obtained by the study is only a generalized one which may vary if the city is categorized strictly as per above strata. Also, the study observed only the current trend, behaviour, attitude, on the spot response of all respondents, be it the consumers, merchants or the banks and did not take into consideration the past trends, behaviour, attitude etc. and the process of change that could have occurred, if any, for obtaining the below said results which are discussed in the next chapter. Thus the results pertain to Chennai city on an overall basis only.

NOTES

1. Arun, K.N. (2007), "At 44% TN is most urbanised", *The New Indian Express,* Express Publications (Madurai) Limited, Vol. 76, No.263, Chennai, November 3.
2. Rakesh Joshi (2007), "Do we need the World Bank", *Business India,* Raheja Group of Publications, Volume No. 770, Mumbai, September 23.
3. Joseph Naujokas (2006), European Card Review, ECR Publishing Partnership LLP, U.K., Volume 13, No. 2.

6

FINDINGS AND CONCLUSION

As the roots of globalization started getting deep, our country witnessed lot of advantages and disadvantages. But one mirror image reflecting the brighter side of globalization is the Credit Card System and its culture in India. More so, when it has its hold firmer in Chennai which was considered as one of the most conservative cities of India, which was better known for its closed functioning. Both tradition and culture, not only being rich but also unshakeable, Credit Cards made this miracle.

With globalization, opportunities enlarged. There were more choices for the people to choose. Chennai city, generally high held for its education level and the policy towards education, and with the inherent talent and skill of its people, which is widely acknowledged by one and all, their ability to easily adapt them to the revolving situation, globalization and liberalization put them on a higher scale and standard. Now, people have more opportunity to earn more. Multinational companies that opened in India, many turning to Chennai since it was considered to have better infrastructure and more so because it was safer to invest in the state of Tamil Nadu than any other state, paved way for their long drawn dreams. This was fuelled by the Information Technology advancement and the increasing number of youngsters opting for it. It made them earn higher, which in turn gave them an opportunity to spend more, to lead a comfortable life, if not luxurious one and to enjoy the worth of being born. People's mentality, attitude, lifestyle and what not, many spheres changed.

With globalization, the Indian markets got flooded with variety of goods and services to be chosen. Global market visualized potentiality in India, an untapped resource market. This led to the *increase in demand for goods and services* in the Indian Market. Chennai City was nowhere below to catch up with this catastrophe as its development was fast, becoming a major hub for many of the multinational companies and hence their products. People wanted to be more westernized. Freedom of choice entered. *credit card culture came to their rescue.*

With the above background, the study was conducted and survey undertaken and the resultant findings of the study through secondary data and from various hypotheses are as follows:

FINDINGS IN RELATION TO THE IMPACT OF CREDIT CARD GLOBALLY AND IN OUR ECONOMY

(1) General worldwide bank credit cards distribution has shown a steady increase, both in terms of volume and in terms of value and percentage.

(2) Issuers of credit cards have been issuing more and more cards every year. This also shows an increasing trend.

(3) Developed countries have already attained a matured market in credit card usage while developing countries are fast rising to the situation.

(4) A favourable economic climate helped in the growth of credit cards globally.

(5) The per capita value transactions through credit cards also has been on the rise throughout the world.

(6) A lot of scope in the Asia Pacific Region, with special reference to India and China has been identified.

(7) Other Asia Pacific countries like Singapore, Malaysia, Hong Kong. Korea is already on the lead in the usage of credit cards.

(8) Cards per bankable population in India are quite low when compared to other countries.

(9) With regard to card spends too, India lags behind other countries.

(10) Growth rate of debit cards has shown a higher growth rate than that of credit cards.

(11) In the credit cards sector too, corporate credit cards has shown a tremendous increase than the personal credit cards. This supports the fact that Indians are still inhibited by debt.

(12) However, both corporate and personal credit card transactions have shown a steady increase in the past few years. There are over 156 million credit cards in circulation in the hands of 5 million people across India.

(13) There has been a steady increase in merchant acceptance.

(14) The disposable income in the hands of the Indian consumers is on the increase every year. Hence there is scope for the growth of credit card usage.

(15) The number of middle income group and higher income group is on the rise.

(16) The general tendency of the people has shown a drastic change. Lifestyle of the people of India in general and Chennai city in particular has shown a congenial atmosphere for opting the use of credit cards.

(17) RBI Report also contends the fact that there has been a steady increase in the electronic based transactions.

(18) Credit cards are no more a status symbol but are slowly becoming a necessary one in the hands of many in Chennai.

(19) Swiping of credit cards for various purposes and items rather than for restricted items has started coming in vogue by the people.

(20) Indian public and private sector banks are also in the rat race of acquiring customers to swipe their bank's credit cards and giving a competitive edge to MNC banks too in the issuance of credit cards.

(21) With the growing importance of credit card usage and understanding its impact, production of credit cards in

Chennai has also begun, which caters to both domestic and international demand for credit cards.

(22) Bankwise personal credit card transactions has been on the rise. HDFC and SBI have shown a hike in this competitive race.

(23) Credit card receivables by banks through its usage show an impressive growth.

(24) People are willing to spend more for comfort. This has been effectively catered by the credit card system.

(25) Education plays a vital role in the usage of credit cards by the people. The more people are qualified the better they are able to update themselves of the intricacies of using a credit card. This exhibits the fact that *structural changes* can bring a vital positive change in the *economy.*

(26) *Behavioural pattern and attitude* towards Credit Cards contributes to the high swiping of the cards by certain sector of the people. This enhances the *marginal propensity to consume* by the consumers, supported by the Credit Card System, throwing light on the *keynesian postulate,* a driving factor for the development of an economy.

(27) Merchants find no problem in accepting Credit Cards in the place of cash. Hence credit cards have become a suitable *substitute* for many transactions for a majority. Incidentally, usage of Credit Cards has also become a *complement* for the Plastic Industry, which has contributed to *derived demand* of various other products too, like the ink industry (used on cards for printing), printing industry etc.

(28) A cut in profits in case the service charges are fully borne by the merchants, is a cause of concern, which in many cases, is noted to be outweighed by the fact that it has contributed to the increase in customer base. Hence it can be concluded that credit cards has been one of the major contributors in the real world situation, to give a spurt to both the *demand and supply functions* in the market.

(29) During festival and other similar seasons like closing stock season, new year, clearance sale etc., both merchants, to enhance sales and banks to enhance their bank card usage, offer various types of discounts to credit card holders which somewhat resembles *penetrating price policy*. In other words, people are able to afford a product for a lesser price than the original normal price, a tactic often exhibited by managers.

(30) *Advertising costs* and other *selling costs* are incurred by banks when they adopt such techniques to increase their bank credit card issuance and usage, but then these costs could also be reaped if they reach the credit cardholders effectively.

(31) In short, from all three dimensions-respondents, merchants and banks, the growth of credit cards and their usage is predicted to be enormous. Such being the condition, higher the usage of credit cards, more transparency in the expenditure pattern in *developing a healthy situation* to the economy as a whole.

(32) There is no significant difference between age group with respect to the impact of credit card usage. This shows that people at any age are willing to use credit cards. This reveals the *increase in consumption pattern*. This in turn would mean an *increase in demand structure*. Higher the demand, higher the consumption pattern leading to more *employment generation* and *increase in income*. This trend has some reflection on Keynes' aggregate demand and aggregate supply function. This is a healthy sign for the economy to grow.

(33) There is no significant difference between occupational pattern and its impact on credit card usage. This would mean that structural differences that might be present in the economy do not hinder the growth of credit card swiping. Hence, more the swiping done, more transparency in the money expended which again an advantage to the economy to grow.

(34) There is no significant difference between educational qualification and the impact of credit card usage. Reforms in the economy have given an overall boost in the expending pattern of the people of Chennai city.

(35) There is a significant difference between monthly income and the impact of credit card usage. It has been found out as per this study that expenses incurred by credit cards become lesser as income increases. However, if this increased income circulates in the form of *cash transactions*, it would only fuel the *parallel economy* to grow which is a clear sign of paralyzing the economy. On the contrary, if it is expended through other modes, say for example, through debit cards, then soon a saturation point for the growth of the credit card industry would be reached.

(36) There is a significant difference between the type of card owned and income which comes as an ancillary to the above perception.

(37) There is a significant difference between comfortable payment of service charges and credit card usage. With continued high service charges, there is likely to be a U-turn in the attitude of the people for opting the use of cash or debit cards. This again may not be explicit when cash transactions take place, adding support only to *parallel economy*. Also, merchants may not issue a bill if not insisted by the customers, which means *tax is evaded* by them. People's money which has to go to the government for increasing the *Standard of living* of the people thus becomes nullified.

(38) There is no significant association between preference to use credit card usage for various items, (durable or non–durable like grocery etc.) and hence people are willing to use their credit cards wherever they feel comfortable. This is a good sign for the improvement of the economy as every swipe and thereby every expenditure is recorded. This helps in the more efficient functioning of the economy as it can help the *Tax Authorities* to levy taxes as per the expenditure level.

(39) It would be worth noting here that our current Finance Minister, Mr. P. Chidambaram, felt that many other sources of income does not enter the picture while computing the tax rates and tax slabs as monthly income in the form of cheques, which are transparent do not corroborate with the levels of expenditures expended by the people of our country. Thus, expenses incurred above a certain limit through credit cards too come under the taxation law, as per the budget.

(40) There is a positive correlation between various factors attributing to the usage of credit cards by the respondents. This underlines the fact that if encouraged to swipe the cards more other than for conspicuous consumption, the efficacy of the economy would greatly improve.

(41) There is a significant difference between acceptance of credit cards with respect to cash or other modes of payment like the Sodexho Pass, Ticket Restaurants by the merchants. However, there is no difference in either accepting a debit card or a credit card by them. In the case of the former, other passes contain with them higher interest charges than credit cards and hence merchants prefer credit cards to them. But they always prefer *Cash Transaction* as it is like a hot cake for them. Such being the case, *tax evasion* and *tax avoidance* could be easily made both by the consumers and the merchants, which is no good for the economy.

(42) There is no association between nature of business and credit card acceptance by the merchants which means that credit card culture has made a deep dent in the *Market Trend*. No merchant wants to lose a business or a customer. In reality, any general market type will be *Oligopolistic* in nature with slight product differentiation and hence every business man wants to capture his share of market. If this is backed by the support of banks by offering discounts to the merchants if their bank credit cards are swiped, he has no hassle in accepting it which will only increase his market share.

(43) There is an association between issuer of credit card and their acceptance. This is because, if the service charges are to be fully borne by the merchants, it affects his profit margin. If a particular bank offers to waive the interest amount or provides with any other incentive, he is likely to accept that particular bank card. This clearly proves the fact of our common understanding, that in any economy, developed, developing or under developed, *Profit Motive* is the main aim of any firm.

(44) Banks, in general, accept the fact that Credit Card segment is flourishing in their respective retail banking sector. This shows the high growth rate of credit cards in the city.

(45) It has also been an acceptable fact that generated statements of credit card swiping show more transparency of expenses made by their customers on using their bank credit cards, which again means effective and efficient governance by the economy as savings rate and expenditures through credit cards are *Inversely Related*.

(46) However, many banks do not want to reveal much as to whether their profits on credit card segment is more or not and to whether credit card debts and frauds are on the rise or not. As to debts and frauds, educating the credit cardholders properly would save much of the banks' time in resolving issues.

(47) Tax payments via credit cards do not feature among the top few in preference rate of respondents. This is in sharp contrast to other developed countries.

(48) From all angles it is quite clear that credit card growth and usage is going to be stupendous in the years to come.

OTHER GENERAL FINDINGS

(1) As monthly income increases to a considerably higher level, there is a decrease in the use of Credit Cards. *Marshall's* law of *Diminishing Marginal Utility* seems to be applicable to the credit card system.

(2) *Schumpeterian Theory* of *Innovation* has been aptly applicable in the case of Credit Card, in this study made in Chennai city.

(3) The current trend of the impact of Credit Card usage in Chennai city is akin to *Rostow's Take-Off* stage. Chennai basically is a traditional city, and the advent of globalization marked the way to the pre-conditions for take-off with respect to the acceptance of credit card culture.

(4) With specific reference to Chennai city, which was always considered as a conservative city, the impact of credit cards, specially after 1991, has caught up quite fast with that of other already modern cities of India, which is similar to the *Convergence Theory* advocated by economists.

(5) With respect to merchant's perception, their attitude of increasing sales by increasing customer loyalty and customer base by accepting credit cards rather than forgo them for the sake of profits which are likely to reduce due to bearing of service charges is similar to *Baumol's Sales Maximization Theory*.

(6) There has been an increase in *Derived Demand* for various products connected to plastic industry with the growth of credit cards. The demand for this particular type of plastic, the demand for inks used to print on the credit cards, the printing industry, the demand for service industry which is an ancillary product etc. have all increased also increasing *Employment Opportunities* of the skilled, semi-skilled and the unskilled at the same time.

(7) When banks or merchants offer incentives or discounts on a particular credit card during festive seasons, consumers are able to avail more with their cards. Thus a situation similar to *"Consumer's Surplus"* of paying less than what the consumers actually pay, advocated by Marshall, can be witnessed.

(8) The study has shown that consumers do make and rank their preferences for a given basket of items for swiping

their credit cards. This is similar to Samuelson's *"Revealed Preference Theory Of Demand"* which states that choice reveals preference.

(9) From the merchants perspective, the study has shown traces of *Kaldor-Hicks Welfare Criterion Of Compensation Principle* wherein though the merchants' could be the losers (due to cut in profits) by accepting credit cards, their loss is compensated by increased customer base and loyalty on one hand, and certain incentives or discounts from banks on the other.

(10) The study shows the similarity of *Externality Effect – Band Wagon Effect,* wherein, many are induced to hold a credit card and swiping it, especially between the age group of 25-40, where usage is more. In certain cases multiple credit card swiping supports this band wagon effect a little more.

SUGGESTIONS

Though Credit Cards performance over the past years has been quite impressive in the country and the general prediction for a wonderful future for this sector is forecast, it should also not be totally forgotten that India still remains a debt-reluctant country which holds good with specific reference to Chennai city too. In fact, the growth of debit cards by certain banks as per various research findings is higher than that of credit cards is a shot in the arm of Credit Card Segment. Hence to improve the usage of credit cards by individuals by personally holding them rather than using a corporate credit card, a few steps could be taken by the Government and the authorities concerned.

(1) To make usage of credit cards more safe and utility based by knowing the pulse of the consumers. It is a general belief among the public that when a credit card is lost, the time taken by the banks to deactivate is more than when other modes are reported to be lost. This would make a fraudulent to capitalize the credit card for which the legal, prime credit card holder is made responsible.

(2) Cardholders should be well educated about Consumer Protection Act and Banking Ombudsman. It has been found that not many go to the Ombudsman for issues relating to Credit Cards for getting their issues resolved and grievances redressed. Cardholders must make use of the facility provided to them in the correct way.

(3) Government can encourage use of credit cards by various segments of people for various purposes as in the case of developed countries like pensions, utility bills etc. This will not only reduce queues in banks, post offices and other similar places, but also make transfer from government much easier.

(4) Enhancing the usage of plastic card which is more cost-effective, for reasons various enables the government to have less paper currency transaction, the latter being more cumbersome.

(5) The charges on credit cards when used in foreign countries are high. If this is reduced considerably, there is lot of scope to earn more *Foreign Exchange*.

(6) In general, receivables in India are high when compared to the rest of the world. If credit card usage is encouraged, there is likely to gain higher receivables by the banks.

(7) The average interest rate and other fees and charges, which is too high in India when compared to other developed and developing countries, if reduced will contribute to higher swiping of credit cards.

(8) India is rich in human resource and equally rich in the earning group when compared to other countries. So an effective tapping of the market itself would improve not only usage of credit cards by the people but also makes the allocation of resources by the government to proper channels easy as every credit card transaction is transparent.

With all the above findings and suggestions, it would be more helpful to us if we better understand the opportunities, challenges and threats facing this industry so that effective methods would make the mechanism function smoothly and efficiently.

OPPORTUNITIES

The popularization of the credit card usage has been attributed to two factors: One, the banks and the card issuers feel there is a huge opportunity in tapping the burgeoning middle income group. Second, from the standpoint of consumers, credit cards or plastic money as popularly known is an instrument of convenience.

(1) Peg the maximum rate of interest charged on credit cards to a somewhat lower level, compounded per annum.

(2) Educate credit card holders on its functions and usage, rules and regulations on usage and the strict terms and conditions to abide.

(3) Ensure transparency by credit card issuers for calculation of interest and other charges.

(4) As far as the banks are concerned, the credit card portfolio of a bank has become a profiteering centre where revenue from interest accounts is high and revenue from late payments, merchant discount and annual fees is also considerably high.

(5) Acceptance of Credit cards by the consumers and the merchants and the banks' eye on sub-urban towns falling under Tier II and Tier III cities, there is high potential of credit card growth. Even in Chennai, the metropolitan areas surrounding the city and the places surrounding the metropolitan areas is undergoing a lot of change and more of modernization and changed outlook has taken captive of the people. Hence there is tremendous potential for the growth of credit cards.

(6) If all banks and other issuers make it mandatory to have a certain level of qualification, regular flow of

income or any other criteria which restricts the issuance of credit cards to holders, frauds, debts etc could be avoided. Quality rather than quantity of issuance, initially would bring lower amounts to issuers, but later, with proper education on their usage, would automatically widen the quantity base too, in a more healthier way.

(7) With increased use of credit cards, the credit card receivables could be considerably increased. In fact, according to industry sources, the banking sector's credit card receivables portfolio increased by about Rs. 46,000 crore in 2006-07.

(8) Not just as a symbol of means of convenience, the *Utility Value* of credit cards should be improved. This will be a path breaking method for the growth of credit card industry. Though much is done by way of co-branding, loyalties, insurance coverage, much more could be done by other means like "SBI Gold and More" card scheme which aim at lifestyle needs of customers. Many hidden charges and other fees including the interest rates could be reduced, if not waived. The loss thus incurred will be compensated by the increase in customer base.

(9) Quality of customer selection will do wonders in the long run.

(10) Apart from the growth of corporate credit cards, growth of usage of credit cards by individuals (personal credit card holding and swiping) would help increase the consumption and thereby the development of the economy.

CHALLENGES

Increased use of Plastic Money in India is fraught with certain risks, if due attention is not paid, could lead to serious consequences for the financial system. The risks are, in fact, very basic.

(1) A credit card user ought to have a standing or credit worthiness to be eligible for a card. Bankers admit that there is no mechanism of credit information on individuals in India, more so when there is a rat race by the banks to add to their list of cardholders.

(2) The delinquency rate in India is as high as 24%-36%. Banks charge a stupendously high rate because a sizeable portion of the cardholders are not able to pay and the others who pay properly have, therefore, to compensate the banks and the issuers.

(3) There is an increase in credit card debt–more and more are defaulting.

(4) There are now many instances of call centre employees for stealing credit card number. Except the cyber state of Andhra Pradesh, no other government (Centre or State) had made an attempt to enact data protection laws.

(5) If not judiciously handled by the credit card holders, interest payments and other charges could seriously erode the bottom-line in the long term.

(6) The race to the top amongst the credit card issuers is primarily through acquisition of more credit card accounts rather than growth-based quality.

(7) The lack of proper infrastructure like installation of Point of Sale terminals, ATMs, (more concentrated in the city), and the cost of infrastructure that has to be incurred pose as a great challenge for the growth of payments card industry which includes in itself the credit card sector.

(8) Credit card victims are on the rise which will hit the future prospects of credit card with an iron hand.

(9) The CSMM–BW (Business World) *Customer Loyalty Survey* has surveyed that customer dissatisfaction is visible in the credit card segment and they feel that they are trapped. This is because of the fact that minute details of various charges and fees levied are

hidden while issuing a credit card and comes out as a devil from the pot when the customer actually starts swiping his card and starts getting his bills.

(10) On the issuer's side, a lot of damage can be done to reputation for those who incur the wrath of the general public or the media. Hence an amicable solution with proper support from law has to be initiated by the issuers in case of default.

(11) Using credit card information during on-line transactions also is not safe fully. There is possibility of obtaining the credit card number and the pin number and could be misused by miscreants.

(12) As has already been stated earlier in the study, though the number of card issued has increased considerably, the number of transactions using so many cards has been virtually nil. It would be beneficial and profitable only if the issued cards are used and not idle.

(13) It is worth noting that it has been the growth of corporate credit cards rather than the personal credit card usage has shown high growth and higher potential.

THREATS

(1) The credit card sector has come in the service tax net that will mar the growth of the credit cards in India.

(2) While banks opt various innovative means to push their cards, cardholders are also becoming smarter and taking care of their expenses.

(3) There is literally no profit to banks if the roll-over system of payment is not utilized by the cardholders.

(4) The interest rates on credit cards are still high in India, when it is getting lesser and lesser in the rest of the world. This will again hinder the growth of the industry.

(5) Threats and other non acceptable methods adopted by issuers openly or stealthily affect the image of the industry and its potential growth in terms of usage.

(6) Deliberately dispatching bills late for imposition of late payment fee turns the customer to look for debit cards which is rather safe and instantaneous. Greed for profits from credit cards would only backfire.

(7) Banks must develop many strategies to counter the increased competition, while at the same time protect its own unique card franchise.

(8) Right to privacy on credit cards is becoming a major threat.

(9) Last but not least, a parallel black-market economy, which is accepted as a fact of life in India, is a serious threat to be attended immediately.

CONCLUSION

Reserve Bank of India (RBI) has made a good beginning in the direction of Consumer Protection and Consumer Awareness with respect to the credit card system by the introduction of Banking Ombudsman specifically to deal issues arising out of credit card transactions. With more and more educated people increasing, knowledge gains power and this holds true in the case of credit card sector, credit card growth and credit card usage by the cardholders. With proper usage, shackling of excess burden caused due to swiping of credit cards by banks and with more infrastructure, credit cards will catch up faster than now with the Indian middle class which now marches with modified outlook. As long as there are goods to be sold and people wanting a better life, the market for plastic money will continue to survive and grow. This is further backboned by the banks and other issuers to supply credit facilities in the form of credit cards to the consumer, and the country's objective of attaining financial powers with every passing year and budget, even brighter days seem to be ahead for the credit cards business. People of Chennai city have shed the debt-reluctant attitude a lot. Also, shedding the mask of status symbol, credit cards have metamorphosised as an integral part of the busy life schedule of people of Chennai. With Western ethos exerting a major influence, the process of globalization and liberalization only adding fuel to the fire to the dreams of the Indian youth, which encloses within itself the people of Chennai too, which has an attitude of compulsive spend, it is more likely that the *swiping culture will sweep the current and future generations to come.*

BIBLIOGRAPHY

BOOKS

Ahuja H.L. (2006), "Advanced Economic Theory–Micro Economic Analysis", Sultan Chand & Company Ltd., New Delhi, Revised Fifteenth Edition.

Amiya Kumar Bagchi (2001), "Globalizing India: A Critique of an Agenda for Financiers and Speculators", Centre for Studies in Social Sciences, Calcutta.

Avinash Jha (2000), "Background to Globalization", Centre for Education and Documentation, Mumbai.

Bhatt V. V., "Financial Systems, Innovations and Development", Sage Publications, New Delhi/Thousand Oaks/London.

Biplab Dasgupta (2001), "Industrial Prospects under Globalization – A Study of India", Jadavpur University, December.

Gibson G. Vedamani (2006), " Retailing–A Revolution in the Making", *The Hindu Survey of Indian Industry*, The Hindu Group of Publications, Chennai.

Gibson G. Vedamani, (2007), "Modern Retailing–Comprehensive Policy vital", *The Hindu Survey of Indian Industry*, The Hindu Group of Publications, Chennai.

Gupta S. P. (2002), "Statistical Methods", Sultan Chand & Sons, New Delhi, Thirty First Revised Edition.

Indian Bank, (2006), "Handbook on Credit Cards", Indian Bankers' Association, Mumbai, March .

Ishwar C. Dhingra, (1995), "The Indian Economy–Resources, Planning, Development and Problems", Sultan Chand & Sons, New Delhi, Tenth Edition.

Jhingan M. L. (2006), "The Economics of Development and Planning", Vrinda Publications (P) Ltd., Thirty Eighth Revised & enlarged Edition.

Kabra, Kamal Nayan (1992), "Financial Sector Scam: Fruits of Liberalisation, Sehyog, New Delhi.

Kishore Biyani (2007), "Retail Revolution–Lure of Huge Consumer Base", *The Hindu Survey of Indian Industry*, The Hindu Group of Publications, Chennai.

Kohli S.S. (2007), "Banking – Imperatives of Going Global", The Hindu Survey of Indian Industry, The Hindu Group of Publications, Chennai.

Kothari C. sR. (2005), "Research Methodology–Methods and Techniques", New Age International (P) Limited, New Delhi, Second Edition.

Nair M.V. (2005), "Banking–Exciting growth avenues", The Hindu Survey of Indian Industry, The Hindu Group of Publications, Chennai.

Oomen A. Ninon (2006), "Banking Reforms--Keeping Pace with Demands", The Hindu Survey of Indian Industry, The Hindu Group of Publications, Chennai.

Ruddar Datt and Sundharam K.P.M. (2006), "Indian Economy", S.Chand & Company Ltd., New Delhi, Fifty Third Edition.

Rupa Chanda (2002), "Globalisation of Services: India's Opportunities and Constraints", Oxford University Press, New Delhi.

GOVERNMENT OF INDIA REPORTS

Census of India & CMDA, 2001.

Payment Systems in India–Vision Document, Reserve Bank of India, 1998.

Retail Banking–Opportunities and Challenges, RBI Bulletin, June 2005.

Report on Trend and Progress of Banking in India 2005-06; Supplement to Reserve Bank of India Bulletin, November 2006.

WORKING PAPERS/PUBLISHED PAPERS /REPORTS

Bairoch, Paul and Kolul-Wright, Richard, (1996), "Globalisation Myths: Some Historical Reflections on Integration and Industrialization and Growth in the World Economy", UNCTAD, Discussion paper 113.

Commonwealth Business Council and Visa, (2004), "Payment Solutions for Modernizing Economies", Global Insight Inc. and Visa, September.

Euromonitor International Survey Report (2004), "Financial Cards–World", Country Market Insight.

Euromonitor International Survey Report (2007), "Financial Cards–India", Country Market Insight, March.

Euromonitor International Survey Report (2007), "Credit Card Transactions–India", Country Sector Briefing, March.

ICMA–The Voice of the Plastic Card Industry, (2004), "Credit Cards, from Novelty to Necessity", Sections 1,2 and 3, July 22.

Indian Payment Card Industry (2001–2006), "Credit Cards", Payments Card Industry, Venture Infotek Research Publication.

Kaushik Surendra K. (1995), "India's Economic and Financial Reforms and its Transformation into an Emerging Market", Institute of Economic Growth, Working Paper 174.

Knowles, James C. *et al.*, (1999), "Social Consequences of Financial Crisis in Asia", Working Paper.

Merrill Lynch Survey Report (2007), "The Credit Card Business : Stark Differences", Banking in the BRICs, Fevruary 28.

NCAER in Collaboration with VISA, (2005), "Development of Electronic Payment Systems in India".

Niranjan Chilpakatti and Meenakshi Rishi, (2002), "Indian Banking Sector Reform and Liberalization: Pain or Panacea?", Ohio Northern University, Ada.

Purwar A.K., (2003), "Banking Sector–Industry Review", Section 2, BSE Annual Capital Stock Market Review, pp. 72-74.

Tae Soo Kang & Guonan Ma, (2007), "Recent Episodes of Credit Card Distress in Asia", *BIS Quarterly Review*, June.

NEWSPAPER ARTICLES

ABN AMRO (2006), "Value For Your Money", *Khaleej Times*, UAE, September 20.

Aurn K.N. (2007), "At 44%, TN IS 'MOST URBANISED'", The New Indian Express, Express Publications (Madurai) Ltd., Chennai, November 03.

Bharath Jairaj (2006), "Right to Privacy", *The Hindu*, The Hindu Group of Publications, Chennai, February 06.

Elda Christy (2007), "Check Your Credit Card's 'Interest Free Period' Before You Swipe It", Your Money, The Times of India Publications, Mumbai, Volume3, Issue No. 72, March 20.

Kannal Achuthan (2007), "Credit Card Racket Busted", The Hindu, The Hindu Group of Publications, Chennai.

Manyara Kirago (2005), "Escaping the Debt Cycle", The Saturday Nation, Nairobi, October 20- November 04, pp.11.

Punam Mohandas (2006), "Plastic Money and its many Conveniences", Khaleej Times, UAE, September 20, pp.39.

PTI Reports, "Tata Group, State Bank launch Credit Card", *The Hindu*, The Hindu Group of Publications, Chennai, February 16, 2007.

PTI Reports (2006), "Railways Ties up with SBI Card", *The Hindu*, The Hindu Group of Publications, Chennai, February 21.

Special Correspondent (2007), "SBI Widens Credit card Portfolio", *The Hindu*, The Hindu Group of Publications, Chennai, August 10.

Subramani A. (2006), "Attention! Credit Card Holders", *The Hindu*, The Hindu Group of Publications, Chennai, November 16.

VNS Report (2006), "Cash Transactions on the Wane", *Vietnam News*, Hanoi, January 13, pp.15.

ARTICLES FROM JOURNALS/MAGAZINES

Abhijit Sen (2007), Business Today–Special 15th Anniversary issue, January 14.

Aditya Kundmkar (2006), "Banking in Future", *Business India*, February 12.

Anand Adhikari (2005), "Banking Ombudsman Scheme: Old Wind in New Bottle", *Business Today*, December 04.

Ashok v. Desai (2006), "New RBI Rules on Credit Cards", *Business World*, January 09.

Banking Advisor for Outlook Money (2005), "Banking Queries", *Outlook* Money, August 15, 2005 and December 31.

Barathi Tamizhan (2006), "Kazhuthai Nerikkum Credit Cardugal", Kumudham, March 01.

Customer Loyalty Survey (2007), "That Trapped Feeling", *Business World*, April 02.

Darren Waggoner (2005), "Youth + Cards = Debt", Cards & Payments–Credit, Debit and Beyond.

Dayamanti Datta (2006), "Plastic Promise", *India Today*, March 27.

Deepika Khatri (2007), "Counting the Credit", India Today–Woman.

Dinamalar article, (2005), "Credit Card, Debit Card, ATM Card", Dinamalar, November 13.

Gini & Shankar (2007), "Puli Vaalai Pidiththa Kathai", Kungkumam, May 17.

Jane Adams (2006), "The War on Cash", *European Card Review*, Vol.13, No. 2, March/April.

Joydeep Sengupta and Renny Thomas (2006), "What Indian Consumers Want from Banks", *India Today*, February 27.

Linda Punch (2004), "Going Abroad–Broad Debt", *Credit Card Management*, Vol. 17, No. 4, July.

Mark Beauchamp (2005), "What you Need to Know before Launching a New Product", *Transactions World*, Vol. 1, Issue 5, January.

Mark Klammer (2006), "The Importance of Local Knowledge in a Globalized Economy", *Cards Asia! Now*, Vol. 7, No. 1, January / February.

Mohan Sivanand (2005), "Wanted! A Fairer Deal for Credit Card Holders", *Reader's Digest*, Vol. 166, No. 997, May.

Moinak Mitra (2006), "Plastic Money–High on Rewards", *Outlook Money*, June 15.

Niranjan Krishnan (2005), "Financial Independence! What's That?", Investors India, August.

Nivedita Mukherjee (2006), "Card-inal Issues", *The Week*, January 08.

Nivedita Mukherjee with Rajesh Parishwad & Dyanesh Jathan (2007), "Credit Cards", *The Week*, June 17.

Puja Mehra (2005), "Restoring Credit", *India Today*, July 25.

Rachna Monga (2005), "Credit Cards–Some Respite for the Harassed", *Business World*, December 05.

Raghu Mohan (2005), "Plastic Smiles", *Business India*, January 17-30.

Richard Rolfe (2005), "Carving up Turkey", *European Card Review*, Vol. 12, No. 5, September/October.

Richard Rolfe (2005), "Russian Revolution", *European Card Review*, Vol. 12, No. 6, November/December.

Sucheta Dalal (2006), "Citibank Ditches Cardholders", *MoneyLife*, July 22.

Sucheta Dalal (2006), "How Good is Your Banking", *Money Life*, September 28.

Sucheta Dalal (2006), Get your Banking Problems Resolved", *Money Life*, September 28.

Sucheta Dalal (2007), "Watch that Credit Card Spend", *Money Life*, Vol. 2, Issue 14, September.

Uma Shashikant (2005), "Spending Spree", *Outlook Money*, November 30.

Ved Prakash Gulati (2005), "Indian Payment Systems–A Revolution in the Offing", *Electronics Today*, Vol. 38, No. 2, September.

Vetcha Rajesh (2001), "Consumer Behaviour", *Business Line– Financial Daily*, July 30.

Vivek T. R. (2005), "A Gentle Swipe", *Outlook*, December 19.

Vivan Mehra (2006), "A La Card", *Business Today*, July 02.

UNPUBLISHED M.PHIL DISSERTATIONS

Anuradha C.V. (1992), "Price Variations and Consumer Behavior Before and After New Economic Policy 1991, December.

Mrs. Girija K. (1992), "A Study on the Impact of Credit Cards on the Purchasing Power of Card Holders", November.

Malathi Shri K.P. (1992), "A Study on Credit Card System: A Comparative Study with Special Reference to Andhra Bank and Canara Bank", November.

Shankari L. (1992), "Bank Credit Card Culture in Madras City", November.

WEBSITE ARTICLES

Business Wire, "United India insures Credit Card Shopping on *Rediff.com*", *www.findarticles.com*

Citibank's Emi Offer, "Inside on Indian Youth : Citibank's EMI offer", *http://youthcurry.blogspot.com/2006/07/citibanks-emi-offer.html*

George Smith Alexander, "Card Spend seen Trebling in 5 years", *www.timesnewsnetwork.com*

Hasan Suroor, "The Credit Card Generation", *www.hindu.com*

Indian Bank, "Handbook on Credit Cards", *www.indianbank.com*

Indian Brand Equity Foundation, "Plastic Gains Credence in India", "Consumer Markets–Selling to India", *www.ibef.org*

Narasimhan C.R.L., "Credit Cards: Compounding Woes", *www.hindu.com*

Personal.Com, "Credit Cards: Gaining Momentum", *http://www.personalfn.com/detailpf.asp?date=4/17/2002&story=4*

Pushpa Girimaji, "Consumer Rights–Cashing in on Credit", *www.tribuneindia.com*

RBI, "Report of the Working Group on Regulatory Mechanisms for Cards (RBI)", *http://www.rbi.org.in/scripts/Publication Report Details.aspx?FromDate=04/23/2005&SECI....*

RBI, "Banking Codes and Standards Board of India", *www. bscbi.org.in*

Saikat Neogi, "Plastic Money, Hidden Charges", *http://groups.google.co.in/group/soc.culture.indian/browse_thread/thread/561ea4a1378e2fl...*

Samir S. Moghul, "Credit Card–Enhance Yourself", *www. mumbai suburbs.com*

Shobha Kannan, "Credit Card Business set for Over 30% growth", *http://www.blonnet.com/2007/07/19/stories/20070 71951010600.htm*

SIFY, "Age of Plastic Money", *www.sify.com*

Standard & Poor's Reporter, "Cashing in on India's Banking Boom", *http://yahoo.businessweek.com/Investor/content/feb2006/pi20060223_239010.htm*

Sumit Bhattacharjee, "Life is now a Pack of Cards", *www.google.com*

INDEX